AIDS

OPPOSING VIEWPOINTS®

Other Books of Related Interest in the Opposing
Viewpoints Series:

American Values
America's Children
Biomedical Ethics
Chemical Dependency
Constructing a Life Philosophy
Death and Dying
Drug Abuse
Euthanasia
The Health Crisis
The Homeless
Male/Female Roles
Racism in America
Sexual Values
Teenage Sexuality

AIDS

OPPOSING VIEWPOINTS®

David L. Bender & Bruno Leone, *Series Editors*

Michael D. Biskup, *Book Editor*
Karin L. Swisher, *Book Editor*

OPPOSING VIEWPOINTS SERIES ®

Greenhaven Press, Inc.   PO Box 289009   San Diego, CA 92198-9009

No part of this book may be reproduced or used in any form or by
any means, electrical, mechanical, or otherwise, including, but
not limited to, photocopy, recording, or any information storage
and retrieval system, without prior written permission from the
publisher.

Library of Congress Cataloging-in-Publication Data

AIDS: opposing viewpoints / Michael D. Biskup, book editor;
Karin L. Swisher, book editor.
        p.   cm. — (Opposing viewpoints series)
    Includes bibliographical references and index.
    Summary: Includes articles that present different viewpoints
on such aspects of AIDS as the seriousness of the problem,
moral issues, prevention, and treatment. Includes critical
thinking activities.
    ISBN 0-89908-190-8 (lib.) — ISBN 0-89908-165-7 (pbk.)
    1. AIDS (Disease)—Social aspects. [1. AIDS (Disease) 2.
Critical thinking.] I. Biskup, Michael D., 1956–   . II.
Swisher, Karin L., 1966–   . III. Series: Opposing viewpoints
series (Unnumbered)
RA644.A25A36477 1992
362.1'969792—dc20   92-19874
                                                        CIP
                                                         AC

"Congress shall make no law . . .
abridging the freedom of speech,
or of the press."

First Amendment to the U.S. Constitution

The basic foundation of our democracy is the first amendment
guarantee of freedom of expression. The Opposing Viewpoints
Series is dedicated to the concept of this basic freedom and the
idea that it is more important to practice it than to enshrine it.

Contents

Chapter 4: How Can the Spread of AIDS Be Prevented?

Chapter 5: How Can AIDS Be Treated?

Why Consider Opposing Viewpoints?

"It is better to debate a question without settling it than to settle a question without debating it."

Joseph Joubert (1754-1824)

The Importance of Examining Opposing Viewpoints

The purpose of the Opposing Viewpoints Series, and this book in particular, is to present balanced, and often difficult to find, opposing points of view on complex and sensitive issues.

Probably the best way to become informed is to analyze the positions of those who are regarded as experts and well studied on issues. It is important to consider every variety of opinion in an attempt to determine the truth. Opinions from the mainstream of society should be examined. But also important are opinions that are considered radical, reactionary, or minority as well as those stigmatized by some other uncomplimentary label. An important lesson of history is the eventual acceptance of many unpopular and even despised opinions. The ideas of Socrates, Jesus, and Galileo are good examples of this.

Readers will approach this book with their own opinions on the issues debated within it. However, to have a good grasp of one's own viewpoint, it is necessary to understand the arguments of those with whom one disagrees. It can be said that those who do not completely understand their adversary's point of view do not fully understand their own.

A persuasive case for considering opposing viewpoints has been presented by John Stuart Mill in his work *On Liberty*. When examining controversial issues it may be helpful to reflect on this suggestion:

The only way in which a human being can make some approach to knowing the whole of a subject, is by hearing what can be said about it by persons of every variety of opinion, and studying all modes in which it can be looked at by every character of mind. No wise man ever acquired his wisdom in any mode but this.

Analyzing Sources of Information

The Opposing Viewpoints Series includes diverse materials taken from magazines, journals, books, and newspapers, as well as statements and position papers from a wide range of individuals, organizations, and governments. This broad spectrum of sources helps to develop patterns of thinking which are open to the consideration of a variety of opinions.

Pitfalls to Avoid

A pitfall to avoid in considering opposing points of view is that of regarding one's own opinion as being common sense and the most rational stance, and the point of view of others as being only opinion and naturally wrong. It may be that another's opinion is correct and one's own is in error.

Another pitfall to avoid is that of closing one's mind to the opinions of those with whom one disagrees. The best way to approach a dialogue is to make one's primary purpose that of understanding the mind and arguments of the other person and not that of enlightening him or her with one's own solutions. More can be learned by listening than speaking.

It is my hope that after reading this book the reader will have a deeper understanding of the issues debated and will appreciate the complexity of even seemingly simple issues on which good and honest people disagree. This awareness is particularly important in a democratic society such as ours where people enter into public debate to determine the common good. Those with whom one disagrees should not necessarily be regarded as enemies, but perhaps simply as people who suggest different paths to a common goal.

Developing Basic Reading and Thinking Skills

In this book, carefully edited opposing viewpoints are purposely placed back to back to create a running debate; each viewpoint is preceded by a short quotation that best expresses the author's main argument. This format instantly plunges the reader into the midst of a controversial issue and greatly aids that reader in mastering the basic skill of recognizing an author's point of view.

A number of basic skills for critical thinking are practiced in the activities that appear throughout the books in the series. Some of the skills are:

Evaluating Sources of Information. The ability to choose from among alternative sources the most reliable and accurate source in relation to a given subject.

Separating Fact from Opinion. The ability to make the basic distinction between factual statements (those that can be demonstrated or verified empirically) and statements of opinion (those that are beliefs or attitudes that cannot be proved).

Identifying Stereotypes. The ability to identify oversimplified, exaggerated descriptions (favorable or unfavorable) about people and insulting statements about racial, religious, or national groups, based upon misinformation or lack of information.

Recognizing Ethnocentrism. The ability to recognize attitudes or opinions that express the view that one's own race, culture, or group is inherently superior, or those attitudes that judge another culture or group in terms of one's own.

It is important to consider opposing viewpoints and equally important to be able to critically analyze those viewpoints. The activities in this book are designed to help the reader master these thinking skills. Statements are taken from the book's viewpoints and the reader is asked to analyze them. This technique aids the reader in developing skills that not only can be applied to the viewpoints in this book, but also to situations where opinionated spokespersons comment on controversial issues. Although the activities are helpful to the solitary reader, they are most useful when the reader can benefit from the interaction of group discussion.

Using this book and others in the series should help readers develop basic reading and thinking skills. These skills should improve the reader's ability to understand what is read. Readers should be better able to separate fact from opinion, substance from rhetoric, and become better consumers of information in our media-centered culture.

This volume of the Opposing Viewpoints Series does not advocate a particular point of view. Quite the contrary! The very nature of the book leaves it to the reader to formulate the opinions he or she finds most suitable. My purpose as publisher is to see that this is made possible by offering a wide range of viewpoints that are fairly presented.

David L. Bender
Publisher

Introduction

"Uncertainty about how much the disease will spread—how soon and to whom—remains at the center of public discourse about AIDS."

Susan Sontag,
AIDS and Its Metaphors, 1988.

On June 5, 1981, the Centers for Disease Control (CDC) published Dr. Michael S. Gottlieb's report about patients who suffered high fevers, weight loss, and lung infections. These individuals were the first to suffer from AIDS or acquired immunodeficiency syndrome. In the succeeding eleven years, in the United States, the CDC has recorded 218,301 AIDS cases. As of June 1992, 141,223 people have died of AIDS. Up to this point, no cure for the disease has been found.

AIDS is spread from one person to another when the blood or semen of a person infected with HIV (human immunodeficiency virus) comes into contact with the blood of a noninfected person. This mode of transmission has left certain populations particularly susceptible to AIDS. The high-risk groups have been and continue to be homosexual men, bisexual men, prostitutes, and intravenous drug users. Because the disease remains largely limited to these groups, most people do not believe it will spread beyond them and into the general population. This has not proved to be entirely accurate, however. A few AIDS cases include infants of mothers who are intravenous drug users, heterosexual partners of intravenous drug users, customers of prostitutes, heterosexual partners of bisexual men, and people who have received blood transfusions during operations.

It is these crossover cases that have some people concerned that AIDS will move beyond the high-risk groups into what AIDS researchers call low-risk groups—mainly heterosexuals. Antonia C. Novello, the surgeon general of the United States, reports that the rate of infection is increasing in the United States for heterosexual women. She states that half of all women infected are intravenous drug users but that close to one-third have been infected through sexual contact with HIV-infected men. Because AIDS has a long incubation period before its symptoms appear, experts such as Novello worry that people in low-risk groups may continue to unknowingly spread the disease to others, beginning a widespread AIDS epidemic.

Others believe this scenario is exaggerated and inaccurate. Michael Fumento, a frequent writer on AIDS issues, points out in the December 1991 issue of *Commentary* magazine that by the end of 1991 "a mere 727 whites, middle-class or otherwise, are listed as having gotten the disease through heterosexual contact—less than one half of one percent of the total caseload." Fumento claims that AIDS will remain primarily within the homosexual and drug-using risk groups. Advocates of Fumento's view charge that government health organizations and gay activist groups distort the spread of AIDS in order to obtain money from the government to finance research and social programs. Charles Krauthammer, a senior editor for the *New Republic* magazine agrees, claiming that AIDS is reported "all out of proportion to its significance since AIDS kills fewer people each year than many other diseases."

Whether or not AIDS is a modern plague remains to be seen. Yet the attention focused on AIDS has made it one of the major issues in the world today. *AIDS: Opposing Viewpoints* addresses the impact that this disease has had on society in the following chapters: How Serious Is AIDS? Is AIDS a Moral Issue? Is AIDS Testing Effective? How Can the Spread of AIDS Be Prevented? How Can AIDS Be Treated? The editors hope that by reading these viewpoints, readers will gain insights and understanding about the debates surrounding AIDS.

1 CHAPTER

How Serious Is AIDS?

Chapter Preface

Since 1981, the Centers for Disease Control (CDC) has recorded 218,301 AIDS cases in the United States. Though homosexual men and intravenous drug users make up the highest number of cases, the CDC has also reported an increase in heterosexually transmitted AIDS. Some claim that this indicates AIDS has become a serious problem for the majority of Americans.

Critics of this view, such as author Michael Fumento, claim that the CDC has overestimated the threat of AIDS to the mainstream heterosexual population. Fumento contends that only 727 of these people have contracted AIDS through heterosexual sex.

Thus, after ten years of study, the debate about whether AIDS could become a threat to everyone continues. Is the disease still predominantly confined to homosexual men and intravenous drug users? Or have new high-risk groups developed? Is society spending too much time and money on AIDS? Or is it ignoring warning signs that the disease is becoming an epidemic? The viewpoints in this chapter debate how serious the AIDS threat truly is.

"The spread of new infections has been proceeding at a faster pace among heterosexuals than it has among gay and bisexual men."

AIDS Is a Serious Problem for Heterosexuals

William B. Johnston and Kevin R. Hopkins

The AIDS virus, once widely believed to be a disease primarily afflicting gays and intravenous drug users, has now become an increasing problem for heterosexuals, according to William B. Johnston and Kevin R. Hopkins in the following viewpoint. The authors state that as heterosexuals become more sexually active, their risk of contracting AIDS increases. Johnston is a senior research fellow and vice president of the Hudson Institute, a policy research organization. Hopkins is an adjunct senior fellow of the Hudson Institute.

As you read, consider the following questions:

1. Why do Johnston and Hopkins see the incubation period of HIV as a serious threat?
2. Why do the authors distinguish between heterosexually transmitted AIDS and heterosexuals with AIDS?
3. What do Johnston and Hopkins mean when they say a dramatic behavioral change or medical progress must occur to stop AIDS?

Excerpted from *The Catastrophe Ahead*, by William B. Johnston and Kevin R. Hopkins (Praeger Publishers, an imprint of Greenwood Publishing Group, Inc., New York, 1990), pages 51-63, © 1990 by William B. Johnston and Kevin R. Hopkins. Reprinted with permission.

It is distressing to note that the number of new AIDS cases in the heterosexual transmission category is now growing more rapidly than the number of AIDS cases among gay and bisexual men. The fact that AIDS cases represent infections that took place five or ten years earlier implies that, even as early as 1980, the number of new infections transmitted among heterosexuals was growing faster than new infections transmitted among gays. It is not certain that the virus will continue to spread as fully through the heterosexual community as it has among gays. What is clear is that the spread of new infections has been proceeding at a faster pace among heterosexuals than it has among gay and bisexual men for at least the last several years.

In addition, it has become apparent recently that the incubation period of HIV may be much longer than originally thought—and thus that the AIDS case data reveal even less about the current state of the epidemic than previously acknowledged. Early reports indicated that most people infected with the virus who were going to contract AIDS would do so within four or five years, with the remainder escaping the debilitating end-state of the disease. Such a long latency period would have caused enough serious complications in using AIDS case data for planning public policy. But more recent findings are even more troublesome. Long-term studies of both homosexual men and heterosexuals infected during transfusion now place the average incubation period at nine years or more, with some people remaining free of symptoms for as long as fifteen years. Hence, people infected today might not show up on the CDC AIDS register until the turn of the century, giving them well over a decade to transmit the disease to others. . . .

Sobering Results

In addition to knowing how many people are now infected with the AIDS virus, it is important to know the distribution of infection among the various population subgroups and the rate at which the disease is spreading within these groups. The government's official position, as stated by the CDC, is that HIV infection "remains largely confined to the populations at recognized risk," including gay men, IV drug users, and heterosexual partners of people known to be infected with the virus.

In the absence of repeated, nationally representative seroprevalence studies, it is impossible to say definitely whether this optimism is warranted. But there are ways to test the thesis that AIDS and HIV infection are not much of a heterosexual problem—and the results are both surprising and sobering. . . .

The CDC breaks down AIDS case data by sex, race, age, sexual orientation, and presumed means of contracting the virus.

Extreme care must be taken in using this disaggregated data, however, particularly with regard to the means by which the AIDS victim is supposed to have contracted the disease. The CDC employs a hierarchical assignment scale that places homosexual contact and drug use at the highest levels. That is, any male AIDS victim who has ever had sex with another man, even once, is generally regarded as having contracted the disease homosexually, and any person who has recently used IV drugs, even once, is generally regarded as having been infected through the IV drug route—regardless of the extent and riskiness of that person's heterosexual activities.

Heterosexual Contact with Persons with, or at High Risk for, HIV Infection.

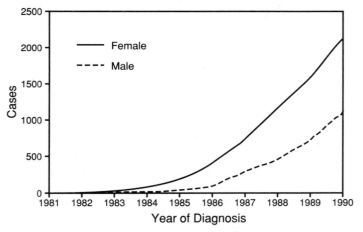

Centers for Disease Control, *Morbidity and Mortality Weekly Report*, June 7, 1991.

As a result, at least some of those people assigned by the CDC to the gay and IV drug use transmission categories actually may have received the virus through heterosexual contact. While the potential number of such misidentified cases is not large, neither is it trivial. As of mid-1988, as many as 3.5 percent of AIDS cases attributed to other factors (i.e., gay sex or IV drug abuse) theoretically could have resulted from heterosexual intercourse—a figure, if all cases were misclassified, that would be as high as the entire category of officially recognized heterosexual transmission cases. And even this is a minimum estimate, since the CDC's risk category for "heterosexual contact" is not identical to engagement in heterosexual activity. Rather, the

CDC's category includes sex only with AIDS patients or those "at risk" for AIDS (e.g., IV drug users or persons from countries with a high incidence of AIDS)—a very small share of possible heterosexual partners. The category makes no allowance for an AIDS victim's heterosexual contact with people who did not fall into these tightly defined "risk groups," even though these other people also may have been infected and may have been transmitting the virus. Thus, the CDC heterosexual contact category is a rock-bottom estimate of heterosexual transmissions that lead to AIDS. It may understate true heterosexual transmissions by a considerable degree, perhaps by as much as half or more.

A second and more frequently noted source of error in accounting for heterosexual transmissions lies in the "undetermined" group of AIDS cases. This category "includes patients on whom risk information is incomplete (due to death, refusal to be interviewed, or inability to follow up), patients still under investigation, men reported only to have had heterosexual contact with a prostitute, and interviewed patients for whom no specific risk was identified." Most of these people may have been infected by routes other than heterosexual contact, although outside experts estimate that as many as one-sixth to one-third actually were the result of heterosexual intercourse. In any case, it is fair to say that, in assessing the heterosexual dimensions of the epidemic, the CDC has taken the most cautious course possible, excluding virtually everyone from the overtly labeled heterosexual category who possibly could have been infected otherwise—and even excluding those for whom no other obvious infection route could be identified.

Heterosexuals with AIDS

But there is a much larger issue, one that is less often recognized. Even if correctly calculated, the number of heterosexually *transmitted* AIDS cases (i.e., people who contracted the disease through heterosexual contact) is not the same thing as the number of heterosexuals *with* AIDS (those people whose primary sexual outlet is heterosexual regardless of how they received the virus). In fact, excluding gay men, who constituted some 63 percent of AIDS cases reported as of mid-1989, the vast majority of the remaining AIDS patients (IV drug abusers, hemophiliacs, transfusion cases as well as heterosexual contact cases) were heterosexuals. And at least some of those men classed as having received the disease through homosexual contacts were predominantly heterosexual in practice. Taking these factors into account, and adjusting the AIDS data for delays in reporting, reveals a sizable heterosexual HIV problem: among the adjusted total of AIDS cases diagnosed through the end of 1988, nearly one-third were heterosexuals. While only about 17 percent of total AIDS cases among whites were heterosexuals, more than half of all minority AIDS cases—some 57 percent of blacks and 52 percent of Hispanics—came from among heterosexuals.

The point is that these people, no matter how they contracted the disease, can pass it on to other heterosexuals. One cannot draw comfort from the small size of the CDC's "heterosexual contact" transmission category for AIDS, not only because it undercounts the number of AIDS cases actually resulting from heterosexual contact, but because it greatly understates—almost by an order of magnitude—the number of heterosexuals who *have* AIDS. William A. Haseltine of Boston's Dana-Farber Cancer Institute has observed, "The infections may not have been acquired by heterosexual sex. However, the patients themselves are heterosexual. To this must be added the statement that most of the people who currently have AIDS and who are heterosexuals have been infected for about ten years and have been transmitting the virus to their partners throughout this period." . . .

A Cause for Concern

According to Ernest Drucker, Ph.D., director of the Division of Community Health at the Montefiore Medical Center in the Bronx, New York, "The initial rapid spread of AIDS among gay men and IV-drug users may be followed by a less dramatic diffusion via heterosexual transmission—one that may develop greater force as a larger, more diverse population becomes infected." Already the CDC estimates that in the next two years, the number of U.S. AIDS cases resulting from heterosexual transmission will increase by 50 percent. Although these numbers continue to reflect IV-drug-related contractions, they also indicate an influx of AIDS into lower-risk heterosexual groups. That doesn't mean that you should panic—but don't throw caution to the wind, either. You don't need a head for numbers to figure out that this disease doesn't discriminate.

Susan Alexander and Jennifer Rapaport, *Mademoiselle*, March 1992.

A conservative estimate shows that slightly less than half of all infections by the end of 1988 were among gay men, who accounted for some 70 percent of whites with HIV but only 24 percent of blacks and 28 percent of Hispanics. The converse of course, is also true: *about half of all HIV infections have occurred among heterosexuals, with the overwhelming share of infections among minorities taking place among heterosexuals.* Moreover, the number of new infections per year among gay men has fallen by nearly 50 percent since 1984, making theirs a rapidly declining share of the overall epidemic.

By contrast, heterosexual intravenous drug abusers are one of the fastest growing segments of the infected population. Already, as of the end of 1988, they comprised more than one-third of all infected persons. The great majority of these infected drug users were blacks and Hispanics, with only about a quarter being white. Still, the rate of increase in *new* infections among this group already appears to be slowing down. The number of new infections among drug users may well peak within the next few years, so this group will represent a declining share of the overall epidemic of HIV infection as well.

As serious as this pattern of infection is among gay and bisexual men and IV drug users, it is becoming even more severe among non-drug-using heterosexuals. In total, a best estimate is that there were at least 630,000 heterosexuals infected with HIV as of the end of 1988—a number several times the top-range CDC estimate, and vastly above the most frequently quoted CDC estimate of 30,000 non-hemophiliac, non-drug-using infected heterosexuals (which is, of course, a much more restrictive measure). To be sure, most of these 630,000 or so heterosexual infections (some two-thirds) have occurred among IV drug users, although that does not change the fact that these people can transmit the disease by heterosexual contact. But the number of infections among heterosexuals who do not use IV drugs is far from minor—a best estimate of nearly 200,000 people. Some 52 percent of these heterosexuals are poor, some 67 percent minorities, and some 67 percent men.

Mainstream Population

These characteristics aside, a substantial number of these people—a best estimate of more than 86,000—are members of the so-called "mainstream" heterosexual population. They are not poor, and they are not IV drug users. Moreover, the number of new infections per year among all non-drug-using heterosexuals has risen by more than three times since 1983, making this group as well one of the fastest growing segments of the HIV-infected population. As Haseltine points out, "AIDS is already a heterosexual problem" in the United States.

How did the spread of HIV infection become so pervasive throughout the heterosexual community? In statistical terms, the answer is simple: as noted, a substantial share, some one-third, of already diagnosed AIDS cases are among heterosexuals, and these represent only a small number of the far larger group of heterosexuals who have been infected but who have not yet come down with AIDS. Moreover, unlike the gay and IV drug-using communities, whose numbers are relatively small, the sexually active heterosexual population is extremely large.

And because of the high incidence of divorce and dissolution of other monogamous relationships, heterosexuals move frequently into and out of the pool of sexually active persons, even if they are at times insulated from the virus through celibacy or monogamy.

There also are numerous avenues by which heterosexuals can become infected. Many gay or bisexual men have sex regularly with heterosexual women as well as with men and can infect women in this way. Many otherwise sexually conventional men engage in intercourse with female prostitutes, who generally exhibit high levels of HIV infection. Infected IV drug-using heterosexuals have as sex partners other heterosexuals, many of whom are not IV drug users. Indeed, a study confirms not only that this transfer of HIV infection from drug users to non-users is occurring, but that it is taking place among the middle class as well as the poor, where the majority of drug users apparently are concentrated.

An Unavoidable Epidemic

Finally, heterosexuals have sex with other heterosexuals. As with the spread of the disease in the gay community, all that is needed for a self-perpetuating epidemic is for a sufficient number of the most sexually active members of a population to be infected and to pass the virus on to others before they become ill and die. If studies such as that by William Masters, Virginia Johnson, and Robert Kolodny are anywhere near accurate—that is, if as many as 5 to 14 percent of the most sexually active heterosexuals are carriers of the virus—then a breakout of the disease into the nonmonogamous heterosexual population is more than a theoretical possibility. It is almost unavoidable unless dramatic behavioral change or medical progress takes place soon.

"There is no heterosexual epidemic and never will be."

AIDS Is Not a Serious Problem for Heterosexuals

Michael Fumento

AIDS is not a problem of epidemic proportions for the white heterosexual community, according to Michael Fumento. In the following viewpoint, the author states that the media and AIDS activists are attempting to lead the general population into thinking that AIDS is a heterosexual issue. Fumento uses studies to show that men and women do not transmit the disease to each other as rapidly as do homosexual males. He contends that the issue has been exaggerated to procure funding for AIDS. Fumento, a Los Angeles reporter, is the author of *The Myth of Heterosexual AIDS*.

As you read, consider the following questions:

1. How does Magic Johnson's case score a coup for the media and AIDS activists, according to Fumento?
2. Why has AIDS funding caused a tragedy for other diseases, according to the author?
3. What does Fumento hope to accomplish by his argument that AIDS is not a heterosexual problem?

Adapted from Michael Fumento, "Do You Believe in Magic?" *The American Spectator*, February 1992, © 1992 by *The American Spectator*. Reprinted with permission.

In 1985, the cover of *Life* warned, "Now, No One Is Safe From AIDS." In 1987, *U.S. News & World Report* told us, "The disease of them is suddenly the disease of us . . . finding fertile growth among heterosexuals." In 1988, the media jumped on a study of infections on U.S. college campuses as "proof" of the long-awaited heterosexual breakout. ABC's "20/20" stated flatly that these were heterosexual infections. (Few reporters pointed out that the percentage of infections was half the rate estimated for the U.S. population as a whole, and that of the thirty infections found, twenty-eight were in men.) In 1990, Cable News Network informed its viewers, "A new report from CDC indicates that AIDS is on the rise on college campuses." The idea was that there had been an increase over the 1988 study. In fact, this *was* the 1988 study—it had taken a medical journal two years to print an article on it, and it was on this that CNN and the AP built their stories. Only with AIDS can an old study be declared an alarming increase over itself.

Media Deception

Could there have been any doubt as to how the media would react when Magic Johnson of the Los Angeles Lakers announced he was HIV-positive? Each year, the press finds something on which to hang its heterosexual AIDS message, to demonstrate that *this year* the wolf really has appeared. Each year it finds a way to use AIDS to sell magazines, newspapers, and shows, and to sell us on the idea that AIDS is a democratic disease that doesn't single out homosexuals and needs an even greater infusion of federal research funds.

This is not the first time the media have attempted to use a single AIDS victim to convince us that we're all at risk. Three years ago it was New Yorker Alison Gertz, who after claiming infection by a bisexual saw her face splashed across TV screens, magazine covers, and the pages of the *New York Times*. The problem, however, was that nobody had ever heard of her. Why fuss over one girl if in fact heterosexual transmission is so very common? Needed was somebody already well known.

Someone like John Holmes, the porn king who died of AIDS. Upon his demise, Holmes's wife told reporters that he got AIDS filming a scene for one of his heterosexual movies. Holmes was immediately heralded as the first victim in the long-predicted wave of pestilence that would sweep through the blue-movie business. But it soon came to light not only that Holmes was a drug abuser and a bisexual but that he'd even had sex on screen with a man who later died of AIDS. While there have been many deaths among actors in the homosexual porn industry, Holmes appears to be the only maker of heterosexual porn films to have died of AIDS.

With Magic Johnson, the media and the AIDS activists scored a long-awaited coup. CNN jumped on the Johnson story to proclaim that now "anyone can get AIDS." How curious to be told that, if a man who apparently had thousands of sex partners can get AIDS, we are all at risk. Marilyn Chase, the AIDS crusader at the *Wall Street Journal*, favorably quoted Johnson's remark on the Arsenio Hall show that "to heterosexuals AIDS is coming fast." One L.A. TV station ran five straight nights of specials on the alleged heterosexual AIDS epidemic.

Not Running Rampant

In the wake of his revelation, Johnson found himself in a position that few people, aside from Tom Sawyer or Ernest Hemingway, ever will: he heard his own eulogy, not once but dozens of times. For instance, in the *Chicago Tribune*: "In Magic Johnson, the war against AIDS has a new volunteer, a superb spokesperson, a fresh hope, a peerless teacher, an almost mystic symbol." ("Oy vey!" as my mother would say.) One AIDS activist gave Johnson credit for saving thousands of lives; a caller on Howard Stern's nationwide radio show said Johnson had probably saved *millions* of lives. To hear the media tell it, Johnson's announcement has replaced JFK's assassination as the event people will recall thirty years from now. Johnson's own contribution was to become a modern Nathan Hale, regretting that he has but one immune system to give for his country. "Sure, I was convinced that I would never catch the AIDS virus," he told *Sports Illustrated*, "but if it was going to happen to someone, I'm actually glad it happened to me. I think I can spread the message concerning AIDS better than almost anyone."

Even as some AIDS testing clinics were reporting a tenfold increase in customers, the media opened the AIDS disinformation spigot wider than it's been opened in years. Thus, the *New York Times* led its correspondence page with a letter from an AIDS activist headlined: "Women Become Top U.S. AIDS Risk Group." *USA Today* reported a Yale psychologist's finding that "women are 12 times more likely to get AIDS. . . ." *USA Today* didn't say what it was doing quoting a psychologist on a question of epidemiology, nor did it say twelve times greater than what; presumably it meant men. One would never know from the *New York Times* or *USA Today* that new male cases of AIDS outnumber female ones by eight to one.

A month before the Johnson press conference, PBS broadcast a show on teens and AIDS full of the usual nonsense that AIDS is exploding among teenagers. (Not only do teenagers have an extremely low rate of diagnosed AIDS cases, but military testing shows they also have a low rate of HIV infection.) The show advised that a single condom can save "hundreds of lives." That would be a hell of a condom, though perhaps I should also mention that one of the show's underwriters was Carter-Wallace, manufacturer of several lines of prophylactics.

© Rosen/Rothco. Reprinted with permission.

AIDS is no more running rampant among heterosexuals today than it was when the media first cranked the klaxon in 1985. In fact, since 1989 the Centers for Disease Control (CDC) has lowered both its prediction of new cases over the next few years and its estimate of current infections. While most of the media insist on using the old figure of one to 1.5 million current infections, the actual CDC number is one million. Since this figure includes all infections since the beginning of the epidemic, which has seen more than 100,000 Americans die of AIDS, the actual current infection figure is less than 900,000. Infection data collected from military applicants and blood donors continue to show that infections from heterosexual transmission remain extremely low.

The reason there is no heterosexual epidemic and never will be is shown by the so-called partner studies. These are studies of couples in which one member is HIV-positive and the other originally is not, and they reveal that, over a period of years, about 20 percent of all women sleeping with HIV-positive men eventually become positive themselves. The only study of partners in which the woman was already infected indicates that of sixty-one infected women and their seventy-one originally uninfected male partners, only one male ever became infected—in what can only be termed a wild relationship, with over a hundred bouts of penile and vaginal bleeding between them.

Every HIV infection is a personal tragedy, but our concern here is epidemic spread. For an epidemic to spread, each case—be it of influenza, measles, bubonic plague, or HIV—must generate at least one new case. Otherwise, the epidemic will slowly die off with its individual victims.

Slower Growth Curves

Where it takes five old cases to equal one new case, as in male-to-female transmission of HIV, you don't have epidemic spread. Where it requires about fifty old cases to equal one new case, as in female-to-male transmission of HIV, you don't have epidemic spread. Occasional heterosexual cases will make news for the same reason that planes that crash make news while planes that land safely do not. But you can no more get an epidemic out of such low transmission rates than you can get a squirrel on a treadmill to provide New York City's power needs. Any epidemiologist can tell you this, which is why the media circumspectly avoid talking to epidemiologists, preferring instead to rely on AIDS activists. . . .

As for the few cases of heterosexually transmitted AIDS that the CDC does list, all that a case in this category means is that the person diagnosed with AIDS *claims* to have contracted it that way. Those carriers who are not heterosexual at all may lie about their risk factors. Nobody claims to be homosexual or a drug abuser who is not, but many who are in these groups are eager not to be identified as such. In short, the number of reported heterosexual cases is not only small to begin with, but probably grossly inflated. A recent CDC re-evaluation of "heterosexual" cases in Florida supports this hypothesis: at least 30 percent belonged in other categories and most of the remaining 70 percent were Haitian, leaving almost no room for native-born heterosexuals.

In their fury to democratize AIDS, activists and the media insist that heterosexual transmission is now the fastest growing category. In fact, all categories of AIDS transmission are seeing slower growth curves, and some have gone completely flat—with no increase. Because the heterosexual portion of the epidemic lags by a few years, it's always been a few years be-

28

hind the other categories in flattening out. Heterosexual transmission has *always* been the fastest growing portion of the epidemic, but it's a distinction with no meaning. What is meaningful is that new heterosexual diagnoses, like those in the other categories, come in at slower and slower rates each year.

AIDS Discriminates

Yet AIDS the disease (as opposed to AIDS the political entity) makes distinctions based not only on sexual habits but also on race. Just as making AIDS politically correct demands that heterosexuals be put in the same risk category as homosexuals, it also demands that such distinctions be ignored. As I have argued since 1987, to the extent that AIDS is a heterosexual disease it is one not so much of whites, in particular the freshly scrubbed, middle-class whites that the media always depict as the typical AIDS victim, but rather of inner-city blacks and to a lesser extent Hispanics, especially Puerto Ricans. Going by CDC figures of those classified as having contracted the disease through heterosexual intercourse, and assuming black men to be no more or less likely to lie about their risk factors than whites, black men have fifty times the chance of getting AIDS as whites. At the time of Magic Johnson's announcement, the CDC had already listed 3,146 black males as having contracted the disease heterosexually. Black and Hispanic women comprise less than 20 percent of the U.S. female population but comprise three-fourths of female heterosexual transmission cases, thanks to a greater frequency of needle-sharing and sexually transmitted diseases among inner-city blacks and Hispanics. (Diseases such as syphilis and chancroid greatly facilitate transmission of HIV from both men to women and women to men.)

As of October 31, 1991, the CDC listed a mere 2,391 white heterosexual transmission cases from a decade-long epidemic. Even on the unlikely assumption that every one of the individuals in question was being truthful about how he or she contracted the disease, that would still be fewer than the number of white heterosexuals who are diagnosed with cancer *each day*. Is it really fair to say that "AIDS is an equal opportunity destroyer" and "We're all at risk" and "AIDS doesn't discriminate"? Or is it more accurate to say that while AIDS should be the concern of all, in the same sense that breast cancer is, that it is nonetheless nonsense to maintain that we are all at equal risk of getting breast cancer? If Magic Johnson had become one of the few hundred American males diagnosed with breast cancer each year, would the media have pretended that breast cancer is a terrible threat to males and patted themselves on the back as men of all ages rushed off to get mammograms? Yet more white males are diagnosed with breast cancer each year than the number who have been diagnosed with heterosexually transmitted AIDS during the entire epidemic. White women, too, have far less chance of getting AIDS through sex than men do of getting breast cancer. Why do the media, the AIDS establishment, and the Public Health Service try to terrify white heterosexuals over AIDS while ignoring male breast cancer? . . .

Lethal Weapon

The other payoff is money. When Johnson uttered that magical denial of risk factors he became a cash cow for AIDS activists. Purses long held open to AIDS were quickly stretched even wider at fundraisers nationwide, and there was talk on the floor of Congress about a further increase in AIDS spending.

Not a Public Emergency

As Michael Fumento has documented in his book, "The Myth of Heterosexual AIDS," AIDS is far from the public health emergency that homosexual groups have contended. Yes, the disease has cut a fearful swath through the gay community. But despite relentless predictions in the press, the disease has not "broken out" into the heterosexual world. According to the Centers for Disease Control, among adult AIDS cases, 58 percent are male homosexuals who do not inject drugs. Six percent are homosexuals who are also drug abusers. Twenty-two percent are heterosexual drug abusers. Hemophiliacs account for 1 percent. Six percent of cases can be traced to heterosexual contact, including those who contracted the disease in Africa and the Caribbean. Blood transfusions account for another 2 percent of cases, and 5 percent are of undetermined origin.

Mona Charen, *The Washington Times*, January 23, 1992.

"Now everybody knows someone who is HIV-positive," says a spokesman for AIDS Project, Los Angeles, in a variation on activists' longstanding warning that someday we'll all know someone with AIDS. Well, I'm sorry, but I don't know Magic Johnson. I never even saw him play ball. I do, however, know Mrs. M., the mother of a close friend. When Mrs. M. dies, there'll be no publicity in the newspaper, though she is loved by all lucky enough to know her. Two Christmases ago, as we sat around the dinner table, she informed us that she used to believe that she could not get AIDS but that, "Now I know anyone can get it, including me." The poor woman assuredly had been chaste for the last twenty years and she used needles only for sewing. But the AIDS establishment had succeeded in getting its message to her. Little did we know that while she sat worrying about AIDS, cancer was festering in her body. She is now fighting for her life, living, as she says, "day by day." If a cancer breakthrough comes along in the next year or so, she may live. . . .

Ironically, the same day the *Los Angeles Times* carried a front-page story about Johnson being used for AIDS fund-raising, it carried several stories describing promising advances in cancer therapy that are being held up for lack of funds. In real terms, cancer spending in 1991 was well below the 1980 level, and that *includes* the quarter of the cancer budget that actually goes to AIDS research.

The disparity in treatment, however, goes well beyond federal funds for research and education. In the U.S., a person who doesn't qualify for Medicare or Medicaid but can show that he's too poor to afford AZT or DDI can receive them free. These drugs, at best, will delay death from AIDS by a year or two. Someone in the same economic position suffering from cancer or heart disease will not have access to drugs that could save his life. The same holds true for diabetics, victims of muscle diseases, you name it. (Other than AIDS victims, exception is made only for kidney patients requiring renal dialysis.) A few days after Johnson's announcement, the state of California, in an apparent effort to placate a gay lobby furious at Governor Pete Wilson for vetoing a homosexual rights measure, made no less than eleven drugs available free of charge to qualified AIDS patients. The state offers no comparable services to victims of any other disease. . . .

Magic Johnson's behavior, both prior to and since his revelation, may have been reprehensible. Normally, one man's acting out of pure self-interest would be forgivable—if his behavior had no wider impact. And it is humbling to know that a great athlete has been sentenced to death by a horrible disease. But it is sadder still that the media and the broader AIDS establishment have turned him into a lethal weapon in their ongoing war against reality.

"If there was a day that we thought AIDS was not a problem for women, it is long past."

AIDS Is a Serious Problem for Women

Antonia C. Novello

Antonia C. Novello is the surgeon general to the U.S. Public Health Service. In the following viewpoint, she contends that AIDS is a problem for all women in the U.S. Novello favors medical research that is specifically geared to finding out how HIV infection affects women. In addition, Novello believes women need to educate themselves about the facts of AIDS, and advocates establishing services that address the immediate needs of women who are HIV positive.

As you read, consider the following questions:

1. Why does Novello believe that women who contract AIDS affect a broader spectrum of society?
2. What does the author mean when she says that men can protect themselves better from the virus than women?
3. Why does Novello advocate women taking care of themselves first?

Antonia C. Novello, address to the National Conference on Women and HIV Infection, Washington, D.C., December 13, 1990.

If there was a day that we thought AIDS was not a problem for women, it is long past. If there was ever a day when we thought women would be only the caretakers of AIDS patients, that day is long past. If there was ever a day when we thought women could not be infected or infect others via heterosexual transmission, that day is long past.

AIDS and Women

There is no more age of innocence with women and AIDS. The Centers for Disease Control (CDC) reports that AIDS is continuing to spread more rapidly among women than men. We don't know enough about the way the disease progresses, the way the disease appears in women. We don't know how HIV infection interacts with cervical cancer, with vaginal infections such as yeast, with pelvic inflammatory disease. We know relatively little about the natural history of AIDS in women. AIDS may well be going unrecognized.

Let me mention just a few important facts. Women often do not believe that they are at risk. From November 1989 through October 1990, 11% of all reported AIDS cases in the U.S. were women and the rates in women increased by 29% as compared to 18% in men. One out of every 220 women in Florida now giving birth is HIV positive. In the United States the overall figure is one woman in 700. A study of HIV among college students, with a sample of over 65% women (78% white), found a positive result of one in 500 college students. What does that say for young women?

As a woman, as a Latina, as a physician I am concerned about women and AIDS. I am very concerned about the impact on minority groups. There are some terrible indications of the way AIDS is hitting minority groups. Consider that the death rate of Black women with AIDS is nine times that of white women. By 1987, the HIV/AIDS death rates in New Jersey and New York Black women, young women aged 15 to 44 years of age were comparable with rates reported in adult women of Abidjan, Ivory Coast—a city with high incidence rates.

We know that minority groups struggle with poverty, illiteracy, and unemployment. We know these conditions are risk factors for depression, alcohol abuse, and many health conditions. Can we really say that these issues are not related to high risk behavior, to a lack of prevention and ultimately to AIDS? . . .

In 1988, in New York City alone, there were 499 Puerto Rican men and 148 Puerto Rican women who died of AIDS. In addition, there were 328 men and 66 women from other Hispanic groups.

CDC funded a study by scientists at Boston University who found that many Hispanics lack even the most basic information

33

about the transmission of HIV. One misconception is that there is a cure, another is that you can tell who has AIDS by the way they look. They also found that a quarter of the gay men they interviewed had had unprotected sex with a woman during the previous year. . . .

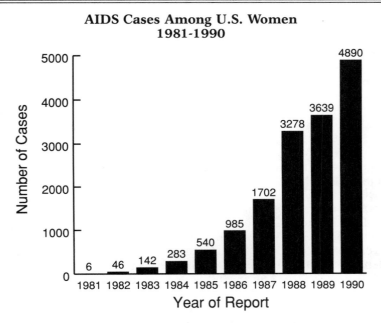

**AIDS Cases Among U.S. Women
1981-1990**

Centers for Disease Control, *HIV/AIDS Prevention Newsletter*, April 1991.

How do women contract this virus? CDC lists intravenous drug use by women, sex with heterosexual male drug users and sex with bisexual men. Then of course, there are the blood transfusion cases, the other known methods of infection via medical procedures, sharing infected needles in drug use, having ears pierced, or tattooing.

I would add that worldwide the statistics offer little comfort and considerable warning. Eight to 9 million adults are infected and a third are women. In Africa, AIDS occurs equally among both sexes. Worldwide at least 75% of HIV infections are acquired primarily through heterosexual intercourse. Over the next several decades, this mode of transmission will become the primary means of spreading HIV infection in most industrialized countries and by the year 2000, the AIDS cases in women will equal those in men.

We must remember that already women account for more than 3% of reported adult cases of AIDS in Australia, more than 5% in Canada, 8% in the U.S., almost 12% in Europe, and already 52% in Uganda.

Often when a woman dies of AIDS, a family falls apart. Consider that worldwide, more than half a million children have already been born with HIV from their mothers and that figure will double in the next two years. There will also be 3 million uninfected children and inevitably, by the year 2000, there will be more than 10 million children orphaned by parents who died of AIDS. . . .

Responding to AIDS

I have seen first hand the way that AIDS touches the lives of women all over the world. I have seen women who are infected with AIDS, I talk to women whose children have AIDS, women whose partners have AIDS, women whose mothers and daughters have AIDS. I talk with women who meet this frightening epidemic head on as they serve as health professionals, educators, social workers, counselors, and caregivers.

Although this epidemic has brought new roles to many people, new caretaking and support roles for many men, women still are the primary caretakers. I am very concerned about the impact on families; the impact on children. . . .

Several factors can severely impair a woman's ability to protect herself from infection, or, if she is infected, protect others. These include psychosocial, cultural, or legal barriers to her decision-making; poverty, and the lack of economic alternatives, with the consequent dependence on a man for support; the social role of women as primary caretakers of children, husbands, significant others, and parents; the well known facts about the lower literacy of women in some societies, their limited mobility, and their limited access to information; not to mention attitudes about sexuality.

In general, it is easier for men to protect themselves against the sexual transmission of HIV. For women, protection is more problematic. By virtue of the fact that a man is sexually involved with her, a woman may not even suspect a man is bisexual.

It is well known that a mutually faithful relationship is the best means of preventing infection. Beyond that, condoms are currently seen as one of the most effective preventive measures against sexual transmission of HIV and secondary sexually transmitted diseases. Yet, many women are bound by cultural and societal restraints from even suggesting that a man use a condom. It may be perceived as a suspicion of infidelity, an insolent suggestion, or even a form of defiant control against the man. In some societies, it would suggest infidelity on the part of the woman. Such suggestions may result in serious problems with the relationship, perhaps even violence or abandonment.

In cultures where married women are traditionally expected to bear many children, insisting on safer sex or refusing to engage in sexual relationships may be impossible because it would limit the number of children. This in some cultures is the measure of manhood and womanhood. In some cases it is a means of economic security and outweighs other issues.

In some parts of the world, women must fear infection when they undergo routine medical procedures. We're more fortunate than that here.

These worldwide trends, these cultural issues can predict trends here. Never forget that this country has many cultural influences, we have women from many ethnic groups. We're not talking only about "other countries" when we talk about cultural attitudes binding women, we're talking about the United States of America.

Women Taking a Leadership Role

HIV prevention is most effectively achieved through women's leadership in the design of policies and the implementation of programs. To accomplish these goals, society must develop a broader understanding of risk, the social factors which facilitate the transmission of HIV infection, the clinical manifestations of HIV in women, and the implications of the illness for women and their families.

New York City Task Force on Women and AIDS, Policy Document, October 20, 1991.

Women must be active and activist. Everyone must see a role for themselves in fighting the spread of the epidemic and caring for those who are ill. I mean everyone. None of us can ignore AIDS. Each of us must do more.

Women must reach out to other women. We must then embrace the entire human family. We must not criticize each other for attitudes that endanger us, or the failure to be careful. We must understand that for many women economic pressures, social pressures are more threatening than the possibilities of AIDS.

But we need to reach women who cannot read, or have less medical knowledge. We need to reach and encourage women who are financially insecure or not able to ask a man to observe safe sex.

36

Prevention is the key to control of the progression of this epidemic. Experience has taught us that adequately and sensitively developed education strategies and programs are effective in inducing changes in high risk behaviors. Women need information on how HIV infection is spread and how people can protect themselves. They need counseling and testing services to determine if they are infected and how they can prevent others from being infected.

The issue of AIDS then is much broader than the epidemic. The issue of women and AIDS goes to the heart of the issue of women in our time. It goes to the issue of how we as women are going to live our lives. Too many women take care of their families and not themselves. We must do both. . . .

Taking an Active Role

We must be active and activist on behalf of women with HIV infection. We need to educate physicians about testing, about specific medical needs. We need to know more about opportunistic diseases in women, menstrual cycles, and cofactors that make women more vulnerable to infection.

We need clear diagnosis of women, sensitive counseling, transportation to treatment facilities, and child care support for HIV-infected women.

Policy makers and care providers must address the entire and true dimension of the issue of women and HIV infection—the individual, the family unit where often the mother is the center and at times the sole caretaker, often the sole support of children and partner.

We need new forms of compassionate, comprehensive care that supports where support is needed. We need day care, transportation, respite care, the finest medical attention, support groups, and bereavement counseling.

We need large answers to this epidemic. Women can't do it alone; the health sector can't do it alone. But women, the health sector, the government and private agencies and the private sector, together can meet this challenge. Our government must have a total commitment to this effort and must be committed to the idea that women are entitled to an equitable share of the resources.

So we are talking about individual rights and responsibilities in a world where women have often been denied such rights. We are talking about mobilizing health systems, research efforts, and broad social patterns. We're talking about political and economic empowerment. We must meet this terrible illness with an approach that matches its power.

"White, middle-class women are more likely to drown in their bathtubs than to acquire AIDS."

AIDS Is Not a Serious Problem for Women

Melanie Scarborough

AIDS does not affect the mainstream white female heterosexual population, according to Melanie Scarborough. In the following viewpoint, she argues that AIDS is mainly confined to those who are homosexual, bisexual, intravenous drug abusers, black, or Hispanic. Scarborough contends that attempts to portray AIDS as a threat to women are misleading. Scarborough is a free-lance writer residing in Richmond, Virginia who writes on various social issues.

As you read, consider the following questions:

1. Why does the author believe that AIDS is not a problem for white heterosexual women?
2. What is the advantage of diverting attention away from the high-risk groups and focusing on white middle-class women, according to Scarborough?
3. What is the real danger to women, according to Scarborough?

Melanie Scarborough, "AIDS Is Not a Threat to Women," May 1992 position paper written expressly for inclusion in the present volume.

There is one way to guarantee you will never be mugged on the streets of New York: Don't go to New York. The deadly AIDS virus can be avoided by the same simple procedure: Steer clear of behaviors that transmit the disease.

Statistically Minute

For women, this is a less arduous task because they face far fewer avenues of infection. The majority of AIDS cases (55 percent) are in homosexual and bisexual men. Gay women are not at risk. The second largest group (24 percent) are intravenous drug abusers—another predominantly male category. Hemophiliacs, almost all of whom are male, account for 1 percent of AIDS cases. An additional 2 percent contracted the virus from contaminated blood transfusions before safeguards were installed.

The only group composed primarily of women is the 7 percent of cases traced to heterosexual transmission. Recent reports have cited this growing percentage as evidence that the disease is "breaking out" among the general population.

In truth, this category is merely an adjunct of a larger one. The overwhelming majority of women with AIDS were infected through sex with an intravenous drug abuser.

Their cases are tragic, but the numbers are statistically minute. Approximately 20,000 women in the United States have AIDS. That's only slightly more than the number who die from falls each year.

AIDS Does Discriminate

The fact that AIDS is spreading most rapidly among drug addicts and their sex partners presents a public relations problem for those who want to portray AIDS as an equal opportunity menace. Gays fear being stigmatized as purveyors of a deadly disease if AIDS does not spread into the wider population. Medical researchers, busy refurbishing their laboratories with the money pouring in for AIDS research, aren't eager to jeopardize their newfound largess. Advertising executives share in the profits by designing lucrative public service campaigns to warn people who aren't in danger of a threat that doesn't exist.

In addition, the AIDS epidemic has created thousands of jobs in education and prevention programs, testing facilities, and statistical research. To acknowledge that the disease is fast becoming a self-inflicted scourge of the underclass could erode public sympathy and jeopardize the tax dollars that fuel this gravy train.

The unfortunate reality is that AIDS does discriminate on the basis of sex and class and strikes minorities disproportionately. Most women with AIDS are working-class African-Americans or

Hispanics. White, middle-class women are more likely to drown in their bathtubs than to acquire AIDS; yet they are invariably the ones targeted by information campaigns.

Upscale establishments provide condom machines in the ladies' room for "protection" in the event of a hastily arranged liaison, even though—statistically—their clientele are in greater danger of being struck by lightning than of contracting AIDS from a heterosexual, non-drug abusing stranger.

A Rare Case

Nonetheless, the media have been diligent in seeking out the rarest of cases—white, middle-class women—and presenting them as typical AIDS victims. One well-publicized case that was reported in women's magazines and recently made into a television movie was the story of Alison Gertz, a white, 23-year-old New York illustrator who learned she had AIDS.

There could hardly be a more atypical example. In contrast to the squalor and anonymity of the ghetto where the disease is commonly transmitted, Gertz was living with adoring parents in a posh, Upper East Side apartment when she made her "single, terrible mistake." At age 16, she spent one night with a young man whom she later learned was bisexual and had died of AIDS.

Alternative Agendas

Certain organizations and groups have specific agendas for not acknowledging just how risk-free conventional heterosexual intercourse actually is. Researchers, for one, will receive larger grants and be funded more readily if AIDS is thought not to be largely restricted to the out-groups of IV drug users (encompassing mostly minorities) and homosexual men but rather is believed to include the heterosexual white middle-class population. Many gay organizations, too, are not unhappy with the warnings that the virus is spreading into the larger community—and understandably so, since the warnings not only spur greater efforts to find a cure but also dilute the burden these organizations would otherwise have to bear of AIDS being labeled a gay disease.

Robert E. Gould, *Cosmopolitan*, January 1988.

In reporting the story, writers took great strides to downplay Gertz's association with the high-risk group and expunge any overtones of blame. Mrs. Gertz reported that her daughter had become sexually active as a teenager with no more dismay than she might have boasted, "Alison was fluent in French by 12." According to Gertz, the evening's relationship was "very romantic; there were roses and champagne"—although apparently not fulfilling enough to extend past dawn.

Readers were supposed to be gripped with sympathy for this young woman who was swept off her feet and is now dying for it. Clearly, they were not to question whether a "roses and champagne" evening is appropriate for 16-year-olds, nor to speculate that girls who get drunk and have one-night stands may be treated less charitably if they live off Park Avenue.

Indictment of Judgment

The implicit message—if it can happen to her, it can happen to you—is a misleading scare tactic. Gertz's case is tragic, but her fate was not inevitable. AIDS is not caused by uncontrollable genetic anomaly, nor is it unavoidably contagious. The greatest risk factor for women is imprudent behavior. Alison Gertz behaved recklessly and the results were catastrophic.

Therefore in women, acquiring AIDS is often a reflection of careless behavior or indifference to consequence. Either she is woefully unaware of the habits of her bedmates, or she knows of the danger and does not care.

No doubt, a woman who has sexual relations with a stranger risks exposure to AIDS. But inviting an unfamiliar man to an intimate setting also places her at risk for contracting venereal disease or being raped, robbed, or murdered. Indiscretion is as great a threat to women as the statistically improbable AIDS virus.

As columnist Suzanne Fields said, "The statistics tell women plainly not to engage in sexual relations with men who are bisexuals, intravenous drug abusers, hemophiliacs, or liars. A woman should know, very well, who sleeps in her bed. . . ."

If she does not, a diagnosis of AIDS is an indictment of her judgment. And it carries an unsparing sentence.

Distinguishing Between Fact and Opinion

This activity is designed to develop the basic reading and thinking skill of distinguishing between fact and opinion. Consider the following statement: "There were 43,339 reported cases of HIV infection and AIDS in the United States in 1990." This is a factual statement because it could be checked by looking at the *Morbidity and Mortality Weekly Report* on April 17, 1992, published by the Centers for Disease Control. But the statement "AIDS is only a danger to gay men or IV drug users" is an opinion. While some people support this statement, others would argue that many Americans, not just gays and drug abusers, are in danger of contracting AIDS.

When investigating controversial issues it is important that one be able to distinguish between statements of fact and statements of opinion. It is also important to recognize that not all statements of fact are true. They may appear to be true, but some are based on inaccurate or false information. For this activity, however, we are concerned with understanding the difference between those statements that appear to be factual and those that appear to be based primarily on opinion.

Most of the following statements are taken from the viewpoints in this chapter. Consider each statement carefully. *Mark O for any statement you believe is an opinion or interpretation of facts. Mark F for any statement you believe is a fact. Mark I for any statement you believe is impossible to judge.*

If you are doing this activity as a member of a class or group, compare your answers with those of other class or group members. Be able to defend your answers. You may discover that others come to different conclusions than you do. Listening to the reasons others present for their answers may give you valuable insights into distinguishing between fact and opinion.

O = opinion
F = fact
I = impossible to judge

1. Long-term studies of both homosexual men and heterosexuals infected during blood transfusions now place the average incubation period for AIDS symptoms at nine years or more.
2. About 17 percent of the total AIDS cases among whites are heterosexuals. More than half of all minority AIDS cases—some 57 percent of blacks and 52 percent of Hispanics—came from heterosexuals.
3. The number of new infections per year among all non-drug-using heterosexuals has risen by more than three times since 1983. As a result, more white, middle-class Americans will be affected by AIDS.
4. A breakout of AIDS into the nonmonogamous heterosexual population is probable.
5. Each year the press finds a way to use AIDS to sell magazines, newspapers, and shows, and to sell us on the idea that AIDS is a democratic disease that doesn't single out homosexuals and needs even greater infusion of federal research funds.
6. Since 1989 the Centers for Disease Control (CDC) has lowered both its prediction of new AIDS cases over the next few years and its estimate of current infections.
7. The number of new infections per year among gay men has fallen by nearly 50 pecent since 1984.
8. As of October 31, 1991, the CDC listed 2,391 white heterosexual transmission cases from a decade-long epidemic.
9. White women have a far less chance of getting AIDS through sex than men do of getting breast cancer.
10. College students are especially prone to contracting AIDS because they live promiscuous lifestyles.
11. The CDC funded a study by scientists at Boston University who found that many Hispanics lack even the most basic information about the transmission of HIV.
12. AIDS will be a serious problem for heterosexuals in the United States.
13. Women account for more than 3 percent of reported adult cases of AIDS in Australia, more than 5 percent in Canada, 8 percent in the Untied States, almost 12 percent in Europe, and 52 percent in Uganda.
14. The United States government must have total commitment to the effort to combat AIDS and must be committed to the idea that women are entitled to an equitable share of the resources.
15. The AIDS virus can be avoided by steering clear of behaviors that transmit the disease.

Periodical Bibliography

The following articles have been selected to supplement the diverse views presented in this chapter.

Robert J. Blendon et al.   "Public Opinion and AIDS," *Journal of the American Medical Association*, February 19, 1992. Available from the American Medical Association, 515 N. State St., Chicago, IL 60610.

Patrick J. Buchanan   "Morality and Magic," *Human Life Review*, Winter 1992. Available from the Human Life Foundation, Inc., 150 E. 35th St., New York, NY 10016.

Marilyn Chase   "Johnson Disclosure Underscores Facts of AIDS in Heterosexual Population," *The Wall Street Journal*, November 11, 1991.

Steven Erlanger   "A Plague Awaits," *The New York Times*, July 14, 1991.

Steven Findlay   "AIDS: The Second Decade," *U.S. News & World Report*, June 17, 1991.

Mark Gevisser   "AIDS Movement Seizes Control," *The Nation*, December 19, 1988.

Nancy Gibbs   "Teens: The Rising Risk of AIDS," *Time*, September 2, 1991.

Marcia Ann Gillespie   "HIV: The Global Crisis," *Ms.*, January/February 1991.

Lindsey Gruson   "Black Politicians Discover AIDS Issue," *The New York Times*, March 9, 1992.

Wade Lambert   "Discrimination Afflicts People with HIV," *The Wall Street Journal*, November 19, 1991.

Mireya Navarro   "U.S. Widens Rules on Who Has AIDS," *The New York Times*, August 8, 1991.

The New York Times   "AIDS Cases Seen Leveling Off in Next Five Years," July 5, 1991.

A.M. Rosenthal   "Silence Is a Lie," *The New York Times*, October 8, 1991.

Laurie Udeskey   "Randy Shilts," *The Progressive*, May 1991.

U.S. News & World Report   "Speaking of the Plague," June 17, 1991.

Is AIDS a Moral Issue?

Chapter Preface

Unlike many other diseases, AIDS has a moral dimension because many people with AIDS have engaged in practices that society condemns. Since the disease mainly attacks homosexuals, intravenous drug users, and prostitutes, some argue that these people deserve to be sick because they violate society's moral codes. This attitude is especially evident in the conservative community. As Patrick J. Buchanan, a conservative columnist, comments: "[AIDS] victims are not victims of society. Americans did not kill these people. Most . . . homosexuals, bisexuals, [and] IV drug users are victims of their own vices." Most who agree with Buchanan see AIDS as God's divine retribution for immoral behavior. Those who hold this view believe that scarce medical funding should not be devoted to treating AIDS. Instead, they say, people who have AIDS should stop engaging in destructive behavior.

Others do not agree that AIDS has a moral component. AIDS should not be viewed from the perspective of who it attacks, but simply as a disease that requires treatment, AIDS activists and others contend. Alan M. Dershowitz, a professor at Harvard Law School, states, "Scientists must not be influenced by the moralistic debate. They should consider the disease as if it were transmitted by neutral conduct." Dershowitz and others view AIDS as a medical and social problem that has been neglected because people afflicted with the disease are often those society considers outcasts or undesirables. The moral issue, say AIDS activists, detracts from other more serious issues such as maintaining quality health care for those with AIDS and providing sufficient funding for AIDS treatments.

Opinions about whether AIDS is a moral issue vary, as the viewpoints in this chapter reflect.

"AIDS is only one by-product of a system . . . in which people have been encouraged to seek intimacy without even establishing real relationships first."

AIDS Is a Moral Issue

Joseph Sobran

In the following viewpoint, Joseph Sobran argues that as the strength of the family has declined, so have Americans' morals. Sobran maintains that AIDS reflects the growing immorality and the acceptance of immoral practices such as homosexuality and premarital sex. Sobran is a commentator on social and political issues and the contributing editor of the *Human Life Review*.

As you read, consider the following questions:

1. Why does Sobran believe that what he calls "the tribal system of control" is more effective than the state?
2. How does the author contrast the safe-sex message of the state to the tribal control of individual sexual conduct?
3. Why does Sobran believe the state is ineffective at controlling the morals of society?

Excerpted from Joseph Sobran, "AIDS and the Tribe," *Human Life Review*, Winter 1992. Reprinted with permission.

When Magic Johnson announced that he was HIV-positive, the public reaction followed a familiar pattern. First the basketball star was lachrymosely embraced as a "hero." He had "heightened public awareness" of the AIDS problem, much as Anita Hill was said to have "raised the nation's consciousness" about the problem of sexual harassment merely by accusing Judge Clarence Thomas of having committed it. . . .

To his credit, Johnson took full responsibility for his own fate. He blamed only himself, and tried movingly to maintain a facade of good cheer. But his endorsement of abstinence was not the message the media were eager to carry for him.

Even so, there was an unmistakable feeling in the air: the romance had gone out of the sexual revolution, and Johnson's contraction of the AIDS virus was a sort of baleful milestone. . . .

False Education

But how much was really learned? The media continued to plump for "safe sex," which definitely didn't mean *no* sex. It meant condoms. Somehow, the essence of the sexual revolution had to be salvaged, though hedged by prudent precautions. New York City's public schools began handing out free condoms to students, regardless of parents' wishes or disapproval. *Newsweek* ran a major article on "Safe Sex," complete with a packaged condom on the cover. . . .

There is something profoundly absurd about this bland pedagogical approach to a medical, social, and moral epidemic. What liberals call sex "education" might better be called *dis*education, by analogy with "disinformation": it can only disorient those who are subjected to it, because it evades what is central. It is explicit without being truthful. . . .

One thing sexual freedom clearly means is the freedom to desert. We speak hopefully and vaguely about "commitment" now; but then, we speak hopefully and vaguely about so many things. We no longer speak firmly of "setting a good example"; this has been replaced by "role models." Chastity is merely negative "abstinence," with overtones of deprivation rather than of consecration to a destiny awaited. To fornicate is to be "sexually active." Husbands and wives, boyfriends and girlfriends, lechers, tramps, and one-nighters are all indistinguishable "sexual partners." If you have the same partner for more than a week, it becomes a "relationship." If the relationship should have an accident, the result is a "fetus," a term that suggests waste matter rather than a human being. (Is there some nebulous association between the fetal and the fecal?) When that happens, the pregnancy can of course be "terminated." The filthiest practices are now "alternative lifestyles," and to disapprove of them—to be "judgmental"—is "homophobia."

Here is where the safe-sexers are at their most dishonest. Homosexuality usually involves anal intercourse ("A homosexual," a friend quips, "is a guy who's interested in the one part of your body you're *not* interested in"), which is less a matter of sex than of sanitation. Most people's sense of hygiene wouldn't permit them to share an ice-cream cone or a soup spoon with a stranger. The mind boggles at the idea of letting a succession of casual acquaintances and strangers penetrate one's backside. And it seems a little bizarre to blame Ronald Reagan or George Bush, as the AIDS lobby does, for any diseases thereby contracted. The question is not so much why this sexual pastime is a sin, as why it is even a temptation. But it has become taboo to suggest in public that homosexuality indicates any sort of constitutional disorder.

Steve Kelley © 1987 San Diego Union/Copley News Service. Reprinted with permission.

This taboo is one more sign of the unbelievable moral crassness that has taken over America. The very slogan "safe sex" equates the most intimate human activity with such handy pleasures as fast food. If it feels good, do it, but wear a rubber. How deeply smart kids must despise adults who give advice like that. Everyone is smart these days, but few are wise. The safe-sexers wouldn't *presume* to give moral advice—not in our "pluralistic society," in which it is taken for granted that kids "are going to do it anyway."

The liberal society has clearly reached its limit, in sex as in so many other things. Liberals may not be prudish about sex, but they are extremely prudish about sexual morals. They persist in stipulating, in the face of all experience, that moral problems are really cognitive, and can be solved by *telling* people things, with numbing iteration, that everyone already knows. "Education" ceases to mean instructing or guiding, and becomes mere ritual; liberalism's last rites. . . .

Society's Failure

The great beneficiaries of the sexual revolution are reckless males and abortionists. Everyone else picks up the tab, but women especially. One waits for some feminist to draw a deep breath and pronounce the sexual revolution a dud; the term "male-dominated" would, for once, be totally appropriate. Nothing is more comical than the safe-sexers' exhortation that we learn the "sexual histories" of our prospective sexual partners before going to bed with them. Could any advice possibly be more useless? Folk wisdom as well as Shakespeare ("I do know, when the blood burns, how prodigal the soul lends the tongue vows") testifies that it is rather pointless to expect an aroused male to be a reliable witness against himself. You might as well ask him if he has ever lied. A girl who is ready to engage in casual sex has already left safety far behind.

Today more than ever, to fornicate is to swim in polluted waters. The risk is incalculable. The safe-sexers are in essence recommending that we play Russian roulette with rubber bullets. They fail on their own narrow terms. More important, they are blind to the real problem. But even conservatives may not be seeing the problem whole.

Laments that family morality has broken down are true enough, but they are only part of the story. It is also true that well-meaning liberals' programs have contributed to the breakdown. But our whole society is becoming thoroughly politicized, and the conservative instinct to call for more police and sterner laws can also be a bogus cure for an extra-political malady.

A deeper insight was recently offered by the columnist William Raspberry, who noted the quiet disappearance from modern society of "the tribe." By this he meant the extended network of kinship, friendship, and hard-to-define "relatedness" that used to back up the nuclear family. Sociologists have called it *Gemeinschaft*, the society one constantly experiences as "mine.". . .

The word "tribe" conjures up images of primitive societies in which men dance in loincloths and warpaint with upraised spears. It shouldn't. A tribe is a kinship system, and it may be highly sophisticated. Elizabethan England was highly tribal in this sense; who you were depended on whom you were related to, not on things like a Social Security number.

In fact, all societies are more or less tribal. Ours is becoming less so. And there is plenty of reason to believe that this is not progress, but gradual disaster. . . .

The state makes statutes and formal laws, but the tribe is the matrix of morals and manners, which are the real stuff of social order. Modern society has lost something vital by becoming more political and less tribal, because the state is no substitute for the tribe. The state can only use force or propaganda, of which "safe sex" is a fair specimen. But the tribe has innumerable subtler pressures and incentives that are far more efficacious. . . .

The Consequences of Abandoning Moral Wisdom

Obviously [AIDS] is a disease tied to specific groups of persons who *define themselves* in terms of behavior that, at the very best, can be called antisocial and irresponsible. Indeed, there is an extraordinary parallel between sodomy and drug abuse: both actions are engaged in for excitement and self-gratification that necessarily reject the constraints and obligations of normal social and familial life; both involve unnatural and destructive assaults on the human body. To gauge the extent to which our society has abandoned moral wisdom, one need only consider that our most influential politicians and public health officials have responded to the AIDS epidemic by attempting to make sodomy and drug abuse "safe" through the mass distribution of condoms and sterile syringes.

R.V. Young, *The Human Life Review*, Fall 1989.

The family without a tribe to support it is fragile. Most criminals come from broken homes, yes, but also from tribes that have dissolved. This is probably why there are so many black criminals: unlike voluntary immigrants, who often came here in tribal waves, blacks were forcibly uprooted from their kinship systems when brought here as slaves. After emancipation, they began building families and kinship-based communities; but by now the welfare state has destroyed them again. It's ironic that when we picture a tribe, we are likely to imagine a black African tribe, when African-Americans have suffered from systematic detribalization at the hands of benevolent as well as malicious whites.

51

The modern state is suspicious of and even hostile to the family, which it associates with "privilege" and "accidents of birth" that prevent the kind of bureaucratized equality it seeks to promote. Insofar as it is even aware of the tribe, the state is even more hostile to it. It sees only the negative side of tribal enmities and prejudices, and has no regard for tribal loyalties. Instead of merely supplementing family and tribe, the state has worked actively to supplant them. . . .

Policing Sexual Behavior

The reason this is so serious, for our present purpose, is that the tribe is ideal for policing the very kind of problematic conduct the state is finding itself impotent to affect: above all, the sexual. The state knows nothing of morals or manners; they are not its province, and it can only act stiffly and irrelevantly when it tries to address them. In the eyes of the state, we are isolated individuals, and sex can only be regarded as an affair between individuals. But sex is a supremely *social* concern, and the tribe has always recognized it as such.

It's only natural that sexual freedom should grow along with the state. To the state's social planners, it is a matter of indifference whether a sexual act occurs within marriage, or even whether it is heterosexual. It's also natural that militant homosexuals should be as political as they are: They want to enlist the state against the tribe's morals, which they condemn as "bigotry."

In most societies marriage is a tribal affair, not just a private mutual contract between the two spouses. The presence, witness, and festivities of the tribe are felt to be essential to the wedding ceremony. Sexual unions are a tribal concern for the most basic of reasons: they determine who will be related to whom. And marriage defines these relations firmly. Tribal societies usually frown on sex outside marriage precisely because its natural result is to produce people without real relations or responsibilities, a fact our society hasn't yet noticed. The whole idiom of kinship sounds quaint among us: kin, folks, misbegotten, bastard—such terms in their literal senses have an archaic or exotic ring now. They used to mean something. . . .

Moral Standards Dictated by Family

As the uproar over AIDS shows, the state simply can't cope with sexual irresponsibility. In fact it has promoted it. For the state to demand chastity of us would be hugely presumptuous, even tyrannical, and in any case impracticable. But the family can *expect* it of us, and the tribe can uphold it as a standard of honor, using ties of affection and loyalty more potent than force or violence because they engage our self-respect as no merely external penalties can.

The state is useful for dealing with egregious criminals who are at war with society. But it can't and shouldn't attempt to police our common faults, which include most sexual vices (in the old sense of sins of weakness). The modern statist mentality can't grasp this. It feels that whatever is immoral should be made illegal, and that whatever is legal, or whatever can't be effectively proscribed by law, should be regarded as moral. . . .

Sexual Promiscuity

At a time when an epidemic of "sexually-transmitted diseases" is spreading throughout the world, public health officials and medical authorities seem bent on de-emphasis, if not outright exoneration, of the principal cause: sexual promiscuity. AIDS is obviously the most striking example of this curious response, because it now is inevitably fatal to its victims—and because its rapid diffusion has resulted from activities that are not only irresponsible and self-indulgent but also immoral and, in most places, illegal.

R.V. Young, *The Human Life Review*, Fall 1989.

Tribal rules, on the other hand, are mostly unwritten, formed by tradition rather than statutory enactment. For this reason there can't be too many more of them than a reasonable person can carry around in him and accept as morally compelling. And for all their fluidity and adaptability, they are more or less permanent. This is so because they tend to approximate natural law.

To say all this is not to idealize family and tribal life, which have their own tyrannies and tragedies. Anyone who hasn't been exposed to their imperfections can get the idea by reading *King Lear* or *The Way of All Flesh*. But a thing can be both flawed and indispensable. Only the utopian will find this a paradox. . . .

Return to the Old Rules

The spread of AIDS is only one by-product of a system that has become too "modern" for its own good, in which people have been encouraged to seek intimacy without even establishing real relationships first. In our society, sex *is* the "relationship." Far from being "outdated," the old rules turn out to have had more practical pertinence than anyone could have realized while they were still generally respected. That they are not the kind of rules the state can enforce doesn't mean that the state should disregard them, as the state-minded have done. No wonder those sexual energies only the tribe can police effectively are now running amok, and bringing death rather than life. And a society that has refused to feel shame is finding itself troubled with an unexpected burden of guilt.

Can anything be done? Well, yes. It's too glib to say simply that we can return to the old rules, though they are pretty much the only rules we can ever have in matters of sex. Even the most sensible rules can't stand up to "the fire in the blood" if they are supported by nothing more than long-range calculation. They require, for one thing, an image of virtue to make them cohere and to give them urgency when calculation takes the night off.

The decay of the tribe, moreover, is like any other environmental disaster. It takes time to recover, like a forest after a fire. Those who demand a "cure" for AIDS instantly if not yesterday are displaying the same quick-fix attitude they bring to sex. But the social recovery will be like a reforestation program, if it happens at all. And it won't even begin until we all understand what we have done to the human infrastructure that carries moral traditions.

"It does not follow automatically that those people who contract an HIV infection do so in any morally culpable sense."

AIDS Is Not a Moral Issue

Timothy F. Murphy

Timothy F. Murphy believes that because AIDS is associated with homosexuality, society has stigmatized AIDS patients as immoral and undeserving of help. In the following viewpoint, Murphy argues that AIDS is not a moral issue, and that AIDS patients are simply people who need help in time of crisis. Murphy is assistant professor in the Department of Medical Education at the University of Illinois College of Medicine in Chicago.

As you read, consider the following questions:

1. According to Murphy, why is the argument that AIDS is a privileged disease flawed?
2. How might AIDS be the result of society's prejudices, according to Murphy?
3. If AIDS is not a moral issue, what does the author think is the moral issue?

Excerpted from Timothy F. Murphy, "No Time for an AIDS Backlash," *Hastings Center Report*, March/April 1991. Reprinted with permission.

Writing in *Time*, Charles Krauthammer described the May 1990 protests by AIDS activists at the National Institutes of Health as a most misdirected demonstration: "The idea that American government or American society has been inattentive or unresponsive to AIDS is quite simply absurd." On the contrary, "AIDS has become the most privileged disease in America," this since Congress continues to allocate an enormous amount of money for research and for the treatment of people with HIV-related conditions. Except cancer research, HIV-related disease now receives more research funding than any other illness in the United States, a priority Krauthammer maintains is all out of proportion to its significance since AIDS kills fewer people each year than many other diseases. The privilege of AIDS even extends to access to certain experimental drugs—access others do not share. . . .

Misplaced Priorities

This view is not new in the epidemic; the sentiment that homosexuals with AIDS were being treated as a privileged class had surfaced as early as 1983. What is new, though, is the increasing prominence of this view in public discourse and the extent to which the view is defended. In *The Myth of Heterosexual AIDS*, Michael Fumento mounts a full-scale defense of the proposition that the AIDS epidemic has achieved national and medical priority all out of proportion to its dangers, especially since the disease will make few inroads against white, middle-class heterosexuals. Fumento writes in self-conscious soundbites: "Other than fairly spectacular rare occurrences, such as shark attacks and maulings by wild animals, it is difficult to name any broad category of death that will take fewer lives than heterosexually transmitted AIDS.". . .

Fumento's book makes the most direct claim that people are dying from neglect because the nation has chosen to worry about people with HIV-related conditions. For this reason he thinks AIDS needs to be put into perspective, but he offers not a word about what priority an infectious, communicable lethal disease should receive as against, for example, diabetes or certain heart conditions, which are noncommunicable and can be successfully managed by medicine throughout life. There is not a word, indeed, on how priorities ought to be set at all. Surely an infectious, communicable, lethal disease ought to receive priority over diseases that can currently be medically managed in a way that permits people to live into old age, a prospect not enjoyed by people with HIV-related disease. It is not even clear that funding should be allocated according to the number of persons affected by a particular disease, since such allocation would effectively orphan certain diseases altogether. Moreover, many of the diseases that do now kill people in numbers greater than AIDS have a *long* history of funding, and the expenditures made on behalf of AIDS research and treatment should be measured against that history, not against current annual budget allocations. It may be that AIDS is only now catching up with comparable past expenditures.

Reprinted by permission: Tribune Media Services.

Perhaps it is the seemingly voluntary nature of infection that invites the notion that enough has been done for HIV-related conditions. After all, if only people refrained from behavior known to be associated with HIV infection, they wouldn't be at any risk of sickness and death. But HIV-related disease is not simply a matter of individual failure to heed clear warnings. Many cases of AIDS were contracted *before any public identification* of the syndrome. Even after the identification of the syndrome, there was no clear identification of its cause or how to avoid it altogether. Early on, there were no efforts to protect blood used in transfusions even when certain screening tests were available. Even after the discovery of the presumptive causal virus and development of blood-screening tests, educational efforts to reach persons most at risk were inadequate and in any case no one knew what forms of education were capable of effecting behavioral change. What educational programs there were failed, then and now, to reach drug-users, their sexual partners, and persons in rural areas. Some persons were infected by means altogether beyond their control: by rape, by transfusion, by Factor VIII used in control of hemophilia, through birth to an infected mother, by accidental needle infection while providing health care or using drugs, through artificial insemination. Because of ambiguities and delays (culpable or not) in biomedicine, education, and public policy, it is not evident for the majority of people with AIDS that there were "clear warnings" that went unheeded.

Even now, when HIV-related disease is well known, it does not follow automatically that those people who contract an HIV infection do so in any morally culpable sense. Over ten years will soon have passed since the CDC [Centers for Disease Control] first reported the occurrence of rare diseases in gay men and drug-using persons. Since that time, ten years of new gay men and drug-users have come along, persons who may not have been educated about the dangers of HIV, young persons who will not yet have maturity of judgment in sexual and drug matters, persons who may not have access to clean needles or drug rehabilitation programs, who may not have the personal and social skills necessary to avoid risk behavior altogether. In some cases there may be cultural and social barriers to protection from risk as well, such as resistance to condom use. It is important to remember, too, that as regards the enticements of sex and drugs, people are weak and not always capable of protecting themselves even from those risks they know and fear. It is not surprising then that a considerable portion of *all* human illness is self-incurred, brought about through one's life choices. This is to vary the principle of double effect: what is chosen is not illness but sex, food, alcohol, drugs, and so on. Their aftermath, unchosen if inevitable, may be illness. But it is telling in this society that those whose heart or lung disease, for example, is related to their life choices are not asked to wait for research and treatment while those whose disease is accidental or genetic are served first.

AIDS Is No Privilege

It is odd that critics see misplaced privilege in the priority and attention AIDS has won where they might instead see a paradigm for other successes. Should the priority accorded to AIDS research and care be seen as an indictment of the wiles of AIDS activists or should it be required study in schools of public health? AIDS activists are not trying to bleed the government dry, and neither are they blind to the nation's other needs. They are merely trying to insure that government and medicine work together to achieve important goals. If other disease research and care is being neglected, the question is not whether activists have bullied the Congress or the American Medical Association into questionable priorities. The relevant question is why other health care research services cannot be delivered with the urgency and high profile that the HIV epidemic has received. . . .

No "Wrong" Behavior

Gay men express their love differently from the majority, it's true, but those who contracted AIDS didn't do anything "wrong." People who were infected by H.I.V. from dirty needles usually committed the "wrong" of being black or Hispanic in a society that offers them largely despair and poverty.

Randy Shilts, *The New York Times*, December 10, 1991.

But all this talk of the priority given to the HIV epidemic is likely to be misleading. It is important to remember that AIDS is no privilege. A diagnosis of AIDS amounts to a virtually unlimited onslaught against an individual's physical, emotional, familial, and economic resources. In addition, there is the burden of stigmatization, given that the disease has sometimes been seen as a punishment or deserved consequence of immoral behavior. For example, a 1988 report showed that, depending on the social category of the respondent, some 8 to 60 percent of persons surveyed considered AIDS to be God's punishment for immoral sexual behavior. A minority of Americans is prepared to tolerate considerable discrimination against people with HIV-related conditions. Varying but significant numbers of persons surveyed report that they would refuse to work alongside people with AIDS, would take their children out of school if a child with AIDS were in attendance, would favor the right of landlords to evict people with AIDS, and so on. Perhaps most tellingly, the majority of people in one survey believed health professionals should be warned if patients have an HIV infection, and a third would allow physicians to decide whether to treat such patients. . . .

One Billion Dollars

All the money thus far spent in the HIV epidemic has not by itself insured adequate medical care for all people with HIV-related conditions. This is most especially true for the homeless who have HIV-related illness. Neither have the dollars spent on HIV research produced any medical panacea. Treatment with zidovudine (AZT) has proved important for some people but not for all, and there are still many unresolved questions about its long-term ability to extend the lives of all people with HIV infection or to guarantee the quality of life. Zidovudine notwithstanding, as Larry Kramer has pointed out, there continues to be one HIV-related death every twelve minutes in the United States. Is it therefore surprising that ACT-UP now chants, "One billion dollars . . . one drug . . . big deal"? . . .

Perhaps the public is used to thinking in terms of billions only for military budgets, but the medical expenditures of the nation are measured in billions as well. The research carried out by the National Institutes of Health has always been enormously expensive, as has been the provision of medical benefits to veterans, the elderly, and the poor. The federal funding of dialysis for end-stage renal disease alone, for example, provides life-saving therapy for only some seventy thousand people, yet its costs have been measured in the billions since Congress decided to pick up the bill for such services. If this kind of funding is any precedent, neither high cost nor small number of affected persons serve as a convincing rationale for limiting the funding now accorded to AIDS research and treatment.

Prejudicial Social Consequences

Budget requests based on what should be done are one thing, of course, and budgets actually produced in government legislatures are another. The question at issue in discussions about the "privilege" of AIDS is the question of what priority should be assigned to AIDS funding given all the other funding needs that face the nation. Richard D. Mohr has argued that AIDS funding exerts a moral claim insofar as the disease is associated with gay men; in many of its most significant aspects, the HIV epidemic is the consequence of prejudicial social choices and arrangements. Because its rituals, laws, educational system, and prevailing opinion fail to offer gay men any clear or supportive pathway to self-esteem or any incentives to the rewards of durable relationships, society has effectively forced some gay men into promiscuous behavior. Neither does society permit gay men the opportunity to form families that could shoulder at least part of the care their sick need. Patricia Illingworth has fleshed out this argument and extended it to drug users as well. These are powerful arguments; it is hard to think, for example, of a single public ritual in family life, education, the media, religion, or the law that dignifies the love of one man for another, that supports any abiding union there. It is also hard to see that society has protected its needle-users where it cannot prevent drug use or offer successful drug rehabilitation programs. American society's enthusiasm for wars on drugs has not, after all, been translated into action capable of helping any but a fortunate few stop their drug use. Needle-exchange programs have been rejected out of fear that such action will appear to "condone" drug use—a fear that is odd given the de facto acceptance of drug use at every stratum of American culture from Supreme Court justice nominees on down.

It is not surprising then, that left to their own devices, many gay men, drug users, their sexual partners and children find themselves at the mercy of an indifferent virus as they try to lead what lives they can. Victims of disease rarely "just happen." More often than not society's choices permit them to happen, indeed make them inevitable. . . .

A Problem for Our Time

The society worth praising, the society worth *having* is the one that will find ways to care and to research, even though there is no formal obligation to do so and for no other reason than that its citizens are ill and dying. The care of those who contracted HIV infection through blood transfusions would be relevant in this regard, as would be women whose HIV risk was a secretly sexually active husband. The morally admirable society would do what it could to protect such persons from infection and care for them when they are sick whether or not society specifically *owes* them this concern and care as a form of compensation.

Subtle Prejudice Replaces Overt Discrimination

In some areas of the country the sheer number of people with AIDS has forced a greater awareness and understanding of the challenges people with HIV disease face. However, although recent opinion polls reflect a moderation of harsh attitudes toward people living with HIV disease, HIV-related discrimination has not disappeared. This discrimination reflects the racism and homophobia that pervade our society and, like poverty, limit people's access to care and compassion.

Report of the National Commission on Acquired Immune Deficiency Syndrome, *America Living with AIDS*, 1991.

Cost alone should not be any obstacle for keeping AIDS research and care a national priority. The research is as important as any other research being conducted in the United States today. Delaying this research will not only impede therapy and vaccine development, but it will also subject the eventual costs to inflation; AIDS research will only get more expensive the longer it is delayed. Delays in researching treatments and vaccines will also increase the number of people who may be potentially at risk of HIV-related disease. It is worth remembering that only one disease (smallpox) has ever been entirely eliminated. HIV-related disease is a problem for our time, and it will be a problem for future generations. It is not something that one can throw a fixed sum of money at before moving on. Even when fully effective vaccines and treatment become available, there will be people who will fail to benefit from either by reason of social deprivation, geography, choice, and chance. HIV-related disease therefore needs to be treated as a disease that is here to stay and not one that has already had its share of the limelight and public coffers. . . .

Too Early to Say

The sentiment grows that AIDS is getting more than its share of media attention, resources, and social indulgence. But there really hasn't been any change in the status of the epidemic to warrant a change in the scope or intensity of research and treatment programs. HIV remains a highly lethal, communicable virus. Despite better medical management, the number of HIV-related deaths continues to increase. More and more hospital resources have to be directed to the care of people with HIV-related conditions. What accounts for the sentiment, then, that AIDS has gotten more than its share? From the onset of the epidemic, there have been many dire prophesies about the toll of the epidemic, predictions that millions to billions would die. Is it possible that critics can say that AIDS has gotten more than its share because it has not yet killed *enough* people? Is the same indifference that first kept the epidemic at the margins of national attention now inspiring the claim that enough has been done? The sentiment that enough has been done for AIDS has primarily been argued in the press or journalistic accounts and not in professional journals of medicine, bioethics, or public policy. Could it be that this sentiment belongs to those who do not know the epidemic at first hand?

If HIV research and therapy are relegated to a lesser rank in the nation's priorities, it will be gay men, needle users, their sexual partners and their children who will continue to pay the price of neglect, and the epidemic will become again the shadow killer that it was in the beginning. In view of the people who are still sick, who are dying, who bear the costs of this epidemic, it is too early and shameful to say that enough has been done. In an epidemic not yet ten years old, it is too early for a backlash.

"The disease is a twisted celebration of an immoral life."

AIDS Is God's Punishment

Donna Ferentes

AIDS is a visible sign from God that homosexuality is wrong, according to Donna Ferentes. In the following viewpoint, she points to her brother who has AIDS as an example of the sinfulness of the homosexual life-style. For her, his wasting away with the AIDS virus is God's punishment for her brother's homosexuality. In order to protect her identity, the author uses the pseudonym Donna Ferentes.

As you read, consider the following questions:

1. How do you think Ferentes' religious beliefs affect her perceptions of her brother?
2. What kind of compassion does the author believe society should show for those who have AIDS?
3. For Ferentes, what is the only way that her brother can find peace?

Donna Ferentes, "Death Control," *Fidelity*, March 1992. Reprinted by permission of Fidelity, 206 Marquette Ave., South Bend, IN 46617.

When I was 17, my youngest brother was born. Thrilled, I took him to the sisters at my high school, who placed him on their chapel altar beneath Christ crucified and before the Blessed Sacrament. In the gesture was the belief and the hope that the baby's truest nature as created by God would develop with grace and in goodness, revealing his true self to himself. Today, I am 47, and my brother, now 29, is dying of AIDS. Although it is terrible to see, he will not face or admit death. The devastating disease has become a last drop into the abyss he has explored for ten years: himself. He is using the disease to deepen his rejection of the true spiritual purpose of his life. A life of use of himself and others as mere sexual objects has left him morally defenseless. The loss of his immune system is the symbol of the loss of his true spiritual center.

A Twisted Celebration

Indeed, in every way, the physical reality of AIDS finds its moral approximations: His wasted body mirrors a wasted young life. The opportunistic diseases ever at the ready to attack him reflect the unceasing efforts of the homosexual community to use the AIDS victim to the end by portraying men like my brother as innocent victims of a haphazard virus rather than as parties responsible for risking and spreading this most virulent disease. In its most macabre expressions, the disease is a twisted celebration of an immoral life. As his lover said to me, "Well, we're all going to die sometime." As I interpreted this, it means that one might as well do what one wants and if it courts and wins death, then so be it. This is an attitude antithetical to the idea that life is a gift to be treasured and which has, for its truest purpose, eventual union with God. Where this is absent, then life becomes cheap, negotiable, a trinket, a bad joke.

In this dreamlike reality, families are supposed to see in AIDS the final "opportunity" to accept their son's and brother's homosexuality rather than to help them to confront it as an accomplice in their murder/suicide. Those families who refuse to play this spiritual endgame and who thoroughly struggle for the repentance of these souls are made to feel intolerant, even cruel, as though they are torturing them with something extraneous, visiting upon them an extra-painful suffering which they should not have to encounter. Worse, there is even the point of view that God himself looks kindly and tolerantly upon their "unions." At all costs, like a lurid skeleton hovering over the half-dead and ravaged AIDS victim, the homosexual death dance must be performed. Its obsessive hopes are to transfix the victim and prevent the family from struggling for the soul of one already totally weakened in spirit and morality. AIDS, because it is so devastating and debilitating, can easily become an excuse to focus on the ravages of the disease rather than on the moment of spiritual opportunity at hand.

Loss of Family

Ten years ago, my brother fled the family to begin a totally selfish and sex-centered life. Fleeing the family meant he rejected finding himself in reference to it; a new identity, wound around the homosexual life, was supposed to provide his "true self." Fleeing the family was a negation of his own creation by God through the sacrament of marriage; the homosexual lifestyle was his repudiation of his roots and the center of his own being. As he lost himself and his family ties, so he lost his bond to the God of tradition and doctrine. In His place was a narcissistic god, a reflection of himself. Every lover was a compounding of this alien god as self.

© Dornfried/Rothco. Reprinted with permission.

All of his "lovers" and the "love" he experienced with them deepened his hostility to the family, and the "straight" world in general. His main contact with the family has been a fugue-like guerilla war. Its main tactic has been emotional bribery: if the family would not underwrite his new "gay" identity, despite the breakdown of his personality that it involved, then the family was rejected. The family had to call his moral lethargy a newly found "good"; his emotional bribery had to be accepted as our own ignorance of the "fact" that homosexuality is as, or even more honest than heterosexuality, no different from marriage, etc. We watched him become less and less human, more distant from us, and also from himself. What he has never realized is that the bunker in which he has lived and defended has had all of the guns trained upon himself. One gun went off. It was AIDS.

God's Lesson

He slips away from us before our efforts can prevail. The dementia, the fevers, the nausea, the disorientation, the loss of memory all seem ranged against us in our relentless struggle to restore him to himself, to us and to God. The totality of the family's love is, through the fact of AIDS, a sign to the world that only the family's love is whole and real. Even if the family universe is not perfect, as is ours, it remains the only one in which the true self as it was intended to develop by God can be found. It is the difficult threshing floor of a happy death.

The devastating spread of AIDS should be read as God's loving attempt to teach His children who have abandoned and rejected His love and discipline this primary, pivotal truth. For homosexuals, AIDS is an opportunity to confront the truth of their moral life. Not many diseases contain this special grace. It is the work of those who believe in God and in natural law to set AIDS in the deepest context possible and not to give in to prejudice against or false compassion for its victims. If AIDS is not soon recognized as a way back to all that is real and whole, if we do not struggle to bring that meaning to it, then it is truly species threatening, for the family and the authentic self as created by God are basic for life in the physical world. And in turn the material world's purpose, including the body, is to reveal and obey God's will for individuals and the whole. Without this, there is no meaning or purpose to our existence or our surroundings. We are only creatures among other creatures, and the very notion of eternity is destroyed by man himself.

"The HIV/AIDS condition does not represent a personal condemnation from God."

AIDS Is Not God's Punishment

Roberto Gonzalez

AIDS is not God's way of punishing behaviors such as homosexuality and drug addiction, according to Bishop Roberto Gonzalez. In the following viewpoint, Gonzalez states that AIDS challenges all Christians to respond in a compassionate way to those suffering from this disease. He does not condemn AIDS patients but rather points out that their suffering can actually bring them closer to God. Gonzalez is an auxiliary bishop for the Roman Catholic Archdiocese of Boston.

As you read, consider the following questions:

1. What does Gonzalez mean when he states that the blood of people with AIDS is no different in substance than those without AIDS?
2. Why does the author believe it is important to disassociate AIDS from the victim's behavior?
3. Why might Gonzalez want the reader to be particularly aware of AIDS in minority cultures?

From Roberto Gonzalez, "Pastoral Support for People with AIDS," *Origins*, October 17, 1991. Reprinted with permission.

Our historical moment is marked in a profound way by the pain of our brothers and sisters here and throughout the world whose veins carry [the AIDS] virus. Whether in the United States, Africa, Latin America or Asia, the blood that runs through the veins of those who carry this virus is no different in substance from the blood that runs through the veins of each and every human being throughout the world. It is no different from the blood that has run through the veins of the human family from the beginning of time, since God created the human person in his divine image. It is no different from the blood that ran through the physical body of Jesus Christ: the blood which he shed on the cross for the salvation of the entire human race, the blood which runs through the veins of our souls through our rebirth in Christ in baptism.

Offering Support

Because we have been redeemed in Christ, we gather ever conscious of the newness of life and forgiveness of sins that is ours; we gather ever conscious of Christ's call that we live as sisters and brothers to all in the Spirit of love, which is stronger than death itself for it is everlasting and given unconditionally by God, our heavenly Father, in the act of creation. Today particularly we gather to reinforce our resolve to ease the pain of our brothers and sisters who in one way or another live with HIV/AIDS, by offering them the spiritual support, strength, comfort and love of our Christian faith through pastoral care. We do so particularly conscious of the fact that significant numbers of our brothers and sisters from the Afro/black-American and Hispanic communities are dealing with this crisis in very personal ways. . . .

Spiritual Life of People with HIV/AIDS

The spiritual quest of the individual living with HIV/AIDS is particularly arduous, because this person has to cope with the acutely painful situation that he or she is enveloped in. Moreover, the individual must respond to this situation in such a way that he or she is able to affirm his or her personal dignity and reality as a person in the face of something that is threatening his or her very existence. The HIV virus, which is still a terminal virus, threatens the very dignity of the person in that it jeopardizes that person's very existence; and one feels deep inside, instinctively, that it is all over.

In the face of this, our fundamental spiritual mission is to say that, "It is not all over! That even if and when I die, it is not all over!" This is the very least and the most basic reality that we need to communicate in terms of spiritual support, namely, that "It is not all over."

With those who carry this cross, we must strive to take our physical, emotional and psychological condition, as well as our spirituality, in order to place these at the service of our personal dignity, at the service of being a person; better yet, at the service of our most fundamental vocation in life, that is, to be a person. At each moment throughout our lives we are called to act like human persons, to be and to become fully human. We can only act as persons within the various contexts of our lives. We can only be fully human by becoming fully spiritual, since this dimension, we believe, is constitutive of what it means to be human, of what it means to be created in the image of God, of what it means to be filled with the very breath of God, of what it means to have a soul.

© Huck/Rothco. Reprinted with permission.

The fundamental context of those living with HIV/AIDS is that of an illness that up until now is terminal. In this sense the spiritual quest and crisis of a person with AIDS is the same as that of a person with cancer or another terminal disease. For fundamentally these are persons who have an inner desire for eternal life, who were created for eternal life, but who feel that they are losing their lives. This is the enigma and mystery of death and suffering. Thus, in great measure, the spiritual task is to domesticate death itself. We must journey in faith with those living with HIV/AIDS so that they think, feel, know and live in such a way that death does not appear to have the last word on the dignity and value of their lives; that their lives are worth much more than that which threatens their very existence; that their lives have an eternal significance which death cannot extinguish. . . .

Maintaining Human Dignity

What does this mean? It means that I will not allow this contact to destroy who I am. For I cannot permit an illness to define or to control who I am. Because I am a person who has been created by God. I am a person. I have a personal identity because God knows me by name and loves me by name, knows and loves me individually. Even though I may not be completely faithful to God, he is ever faithful to me. Because of this I will always be a person, loved by God. Even if I am to become reduced to a state of barely existing; and even if the only thing that remains in my life is my own limited knowledge of God or perhaps, and even more important, God's knowledge of me; if God knows me, nothing can destroy me; for in this I already begin to experience and to have eternal life, the fullness of life and time.

My dignity as a person consists in that I have been thought of, have been known and have been sustained in my identity by God, who has created me in the image and likeness of his only begotten Son, Jesus Christ, the firstborn from the dead. It is vital to reaffirm this dignity to those living with HIV/AIDS.

On account of this none of us can permit any earthly reality to control or to obliterate me. This is why St. Paul would write in his Letter to the Romans, Chapter 8, verses 35-39, that nothing can separate us from the love of God in Christ Jesus.

> Who will separate us from the love of Christ? Trial, or distress, or persecution, or hunger, or nakedness, or danger, or the sword? As Scripture says, "For your sake we are being slain all the day long; we are looked upon as sheep to be slaughtered." Yet in all this we are more than conquerors because of him who has loved us. For I am certain that neither death nor life, neither angels nor principalities, neither the present nor the future, nor powers, neither height nor depth nor any other creature, will be able to separate us from the love of God that comes to us in Christ Jesus, our Lord.

Spiritually, someone who is living with HIV/AIDS must respond to his or her reality like any person who is affected with a terminal illness, by translating these words of St. Paul into the very substance of their lives; in short, by making these words of

St. Paul their very own. Nothing can separate me from the love of God, neither illness, nor death, nor the future, nor the past, nothing can separate us from the love of God that is ours in Christ. This is also the spiritual mission of each follower of Jesus in life.

Responding to God's Love

However, on the one hand, while HIV/AIDS is like any other terminal illness and underscores our universal human suffering in the face of death, on the other hand it is unique in the manner in which it marks the majority of those actually living with this virus because of the ways in which it is more frequently acquired, thus intensifying for these individuals the vulnerability of their human histories. For there are certain particular characteristics that surround the HIV/AIDS condition, circumstances which are particularly dramatic for a Christian, which weigh upon our consciences. . . .

This situation poses particular problems within society; thus the need, for example, to demythologize the fears of those who think that the virus can be transmitted through ordinary, casual, familiar human contact.

Responding to People with AIDS

Stories of persons with AIDS must not become occasions for stereotyping or prejudice, for anger or recrimination, for rejection or isolation, for injustice or condemnation. They provide us with an opportunity to walk with those who are suffering, to be compassionate toward those whom we might otherwise fear, to bring strength and courage both to those who face the prospect of dying as well as to their loved ones.

U.S. Catholic Conference Administrative Board, *The Many Faces of AIDS: A Gospel Response*, November 1987.

It also poses certain difficulties within the individuals themselves living and coping with this condition in their hearts and consciences in the quest for inner peace and joy. It fosters reflection upon the circumstances of one's life and the consequence of one's actions, as though to say to oneself, "If I had not acted in certain ways, probably I would not find myself in this present situation."

This is precisely why these persons are very challenging and difficult spiritual cases. If this were not so, there would not be anything radically new about HIV/AIDS and about coping with this, because then it would be like coping with any other illness that directly threatens our very lives; and those with HIV/AIDS

71

would face the same kind of situation that confronts any human person who is terminally ill. To state it in a different way, the person living with HIV/AIDS would not be in the present predicament if certain choices had not been made, and this, I believe, is at the root of the spiritual crisis that unsettles the hearts and souls of our brothers and sisters in Christ who are living with HIV/AIDS.

This is why some may ask aloud or wonder, "Is this a punishment from God?" This is the most severe spiritual problem, and the one that requires the most support from us to those living with HIV/AIDS. This is the dark night of the soul of these brothers and sisters of ours.

A Trial of Life

In their soliloquy as well as in their colloquy with God, I can hear our brothers and sisters say to themselves, "But I have been a good person. I have helped others. I have been a religious person." An addict may add, "I lost control of myself to dependencies in order to cope with stress or rejection." A homosexual may add, "I was trying to respond to my needs for love, because I am physical." Both may say, "I was simply looking for happiness in life, as everyone is trying to do. Now it seems like I have been condemned because of who I am." A hemophiliac may say, "This condition has fallen upon me completely by accident? Why?" Likewise, a faithful spouse.

These are very sensitive issues and complex matters. And you might think that I should not have mentioned these examples. However, this is, I think, where our spiritual support and guidance is most needed, because in our deepest selves and consciences these are the matters, the moral ones, and their relation to our spiritual lives, that are in most need of healing and reconciliation.

God's Grace

Rooted in the teachings of our faith, we need to communicate that the HIV/AIDS condition does not represent a personal condemnation from God, but that it is, like every major or minor trial in life, an opportunity to cooperate with God's amazing and redemptive grace so as to grow personally in holiness and to live more fully in Jesus Christ. Our spiritual support must strive to enable those living with HIV/AIDS to experience new purpose and resolve in their lives, namely, to appreciate that their lives are worth living, that they are needed, that they are loved by us with the love of God, that in Christ we have newness of life and forgiveness of sins.

Distinguishing Bias from Reason

When dealing with controversial subjects many people allow their emotions to dominate their powers of reason. Thus, one of the most important critical thinking skills is the ability to distinguish between statements based upon emotion or bias and those based upon a rational consideration of the facts. For example, consider the following statement: "The liberal media exaggerates the problem of AIDS." This statement is biased. The author is basing his opinion on an emotional, unsubstantiated belief that the media exaggerates social problems. In contrast, the statement, "When the media latch on to a particular issue like AIDS, they often exaggerate its importance" is a reasonable statement. Excessive media coverage of one issue can affect how the public perceives the issue. The author is using this fact to substantiate his opinion.

Another element the reader should take into account is whether an author has a personal or professional stake in advancing a particular opinion. For example, the manufacturer of an AIDS drug may defend the drug's high price. Since it is in the interest of pharmaceutical manufacturers to make a profit, the reader should ask whether this business interest influences the author's statement. A critical reader should always be alert to an author's background and credentials when attempting to identify bias. Note also that it is possible to have a strong interest in a subject and still present an objective case. A researcher who has been studying and charting the spread of AIDS in the general population is in an excellent position to estimate how it might impact the general population in the future.

The following statements are adapted from opinions expressed in the viewpoints in this chapter. Consider each statement carefully. *Mark R for any statement you believe is based on reason or a rational consideration of the facts. Mark B for any statement you believe is based on bias, prejudice, or emotion. Mark I for any statement you think is impossible to judge.*

If you are doing this activity as a member of a class or group, compare your answers with those of others. Be able to defend your answers. You may discover that others come to different conclusions than you do. Listening to the rationale others present for their answers may give you valuable insights in distinguishing between bias and reason.

> R = *a statement based upon reason*
> B = *a statement based upon bias*
> I = *a statement impossible to judge*

1. Sexual freedom clearly means the freedom to desert your spouse once you are sexually attracted to someone else.
2. The great beneficiaries of the sexual revolution are reckless males and abortionists.
3. When a family is strong it can influence the morals of individual members within the family.
4. Because homosexuals engage in sexual practices that cause AIDS, they have only themselves to blame if they acquire the disease.
5. Homosexuals with AIDS are being treated as a privileged class.
6. People are weak and not capable of protecting themselves from the enticements of sex and drugs.
7. If people refrained from behavior known to be associated with HIV infection, they would not be at any risk of getting AIDS.
8. Society's rituals, laws, educational system, and prevailing opinion fail to support gay men's self-esteem or to offer incentives to durable relationships. Therefore, society has forced some gay men into promiscuous relationships.
9. Only the traditional family's love can instill moral character.
10. The homosexual life-style is a repudiation of one's family ties and connection to God.
11. Homosexuals with AIDS must confront the fact that their life-style puts them at risk for the disease.
12. Since people with AIDS face a terminal disease, their spiritual journey is the same as that of a person with cancer or any other terminal disease.
13. A person would not be sick with AIDS if they had not been a practicing homosexual or intravenous drug user.
14. The blood of AIDS victims is no different in substance from the blood that runs in every human being who does not have HIV.

Periodical Bibliography

The following articles have been selected to supplement the diverse views presented in this chapter.

Robert Bazell — "Happy Campers," *The New Republic*, March 9, 1992.

Katherine Boo — "What Mother Theresa Could Learn in a Leather Bar," *Washington Monthly*, June 1991.

Mona Charen — "Are Heterosexuals Responsible for AIDS?" *Conservative Chronicle*, July 11, 1990.

Mona Charen — "Other Victims Don't Stage Protest," *Conservative Chronicle*, June 19, 1991. Available from PO Box 11297, Des Moines, IA 50340-1297.

Virginia M. Conlon — "AIDS Happened to Us All," *St. Anthony Messenger*, August 1991. Available from the Franciscan Friars of St. John the Baptist Province, 1615 Republic St., Cincinnati, OH 45210.

Michael S. Gottlieb — "AIDS — The Second Decade," *The New York Times*, June 5, 1991.

Barbara Grizzuti Harrison — "Do You Believe in Magic?" *Mademoiselle*, March 1992.

Jeffrey Hart — "Why Has AIDS Become So Chic?" *Conservative Chronicle*, January 9, 1991.

Paul Harvey — "Our Most 'Politicized' Disease," *Conservative Chronicle*, March 18, 1992.

Joe Nangle — "The AIDS Pandemic: Challenge to the Church," *Sojourners*, June 1992.

Religion and Society Report — "A Disease Like Any Other . . . ," October 1991. Available from PO Box 424, Mt. Morris, IL 61054.

Phyllis Schlafly — "Somebody Has Sold Magic a Bill of Goods," *Conservative Chronicle*, December 11, 1991.

Sarah Schulman — "Getting Normal," *Mother Jones*, April 1992.

Robert E. Sullivan Jr. — "The AIDS Monster," *Mademoiselle*, April 1992.

Is AIDS Testing
Effective?

Chapter Preface

Kimberly Bergalis made a routine visit to her dentist in the summer of 1987. Unknown to her, the dentist had AIDS. In November of 1989 Bergalis was diagnosed as having AIDS. She had contracted it from the dentist during an invasive medical procedure. On December·12, 1991, she died. Before her death, Bergalis made several poignant public pleas for mandatory AIDS testing of health care professionals. Bergalis argued that this information should be made public so that no one else would have to suffer her fate. Many members of the public agreed and were dismayed to discover that no current mandatory testing program was in place. An outcry for mandatory testing and the publication of the results ensued. Opponents said the Bergalis case exploited the public's fear. It was an unusual case, they said, and should not be used to justify widespread mandatory testing which might violate civil rights, especially the right to privacy.

Those who support testing argue that AIDS should be treated no differently than any other infectious disease. When venereal diseases or hepatitis are reported, for example, all people who had high-risk contact with the infected person are tracked down and tested or treated. This prevents the disease from spreading further and also makes sure that those in danger of catching the disease are treated quickly. Treating AIDS differently, many argue, leaves innocent people at risk and increases the likelihood of even more people contracting the disease.

Some experts disagree vehemently with this perspective. AIDS is not like any other disease, they argue. Its stigma is far more serious than that of any other infectious disease. People with AIDS are discriminated against in housing, employment, and in numerous other ways. Mandatory testing and publication of the results would lead to more extensive discrimination. Critics also argue that testing would not work because many who suspect they might have AIDS would not be tested for fear the results would be made public. This would lead to far more cases of AIDS than occur now because these afflicted individuals might continue high-risk behavior, thereby infecting others. In addition, those who are HIV positive but have no symptoms would miss the chance for early treatment.

The issue of public health versus civil rights runs strongly through the debates that follow. Whether it is possible to protect the public from AIDS and at the same time protect the privacy of those afflicted with the AIDS virus is a difficult and controversial issue.

"Health-care professionals involved in invasive procedures should have mandatory testing for HIV."

Health Care Workers Should Be Tested for HIV

William E. Dannemeyer and Sanford F. Kuvin

William E. Dannemeyer is a U.S. representative from California and the senior Republican on the House Energy and Commerce Committee's Subcommittee on Health and the Environment. In Part I of the following viewpoint, Dannemeyer contends that mandatory testing of health care workers will protect people from AIDS. In Part II, Sanford F. Kuvin believes that because precautions against infection are not enough to prevent the spread of AIDS, medical personnel who perform invasive procedures have a duty to test themselves and make their status available to their patients. Kuvin, a professor of medicine at the University of Miami School of Medicine, is vice chairman of the National Foundation for Infectious Diseases.

As you read, consider the following questions:

1. According to Dannemeyer, what reasons justify mandatory testing of health care workers for HIV?
2. What are seven ways that health care professionals can respond to AIDS, according to Kuvin?
3. Which article do you think presents the more compelling reason for testing health care workers? Why?

William E. Dannemeyer, "Voluntarism Failed Kimberly Bergalis," statement before the U.S. House Committee on Energy and Commerce, subcommittee on Health and the Environment, 1991. Sanford F. Kuvin, "Doctors with HIV Do Pose a Risk," *The Philadelphia Inquirer*, February 3, 1991. Dr. Kuvin's views on this topic are not shared by the National Foundation for Infectious Diseases.

I

Your wife is about to deliver and is rushed to the hospital into the waiting arms of an obstetrician/gynecologist who is infected with the AIDS virus. Although this physician has two lesions on the back of his right hand that are AIDS-related, he scrupulously follows "universal precautions" and wears latex gloves whenever he delivers babies. Do you and your wife have a right to know of this physician's condition *before* rushing into the delivery room?

The overwhelming majority of Americans, and most of their physicians, believe that they have that right. Tragically, the federal Centers for Disease Control (CDC), the American Medical Association (AMA), and other powerful special interest groups would deny you this right.

American Public Wants Testing

Rarely do more than 90% of the American people agree on anything, but an ABC News survey reported that 92% of Americans want the government to require AIDS tests for doctors who perform surgery, 96% want AIDS-infected doctors and dentists to notify their patients before surgery, and 96% feel that patients who are infected with AIDS should notify their health care providers prior to an invasive procedure.

Interestingly, most health care providers agree. A Columbia University survey of physicians and registered nurses found that 57% of the doctors and 63% of the nurses support mandatory AIDS tests for health care workers who perform invasive medical and dental procedures.

But, unfortunately, some of the estimated 50,000 health care workers who are infected with AIDS seem determined to hide their infection. A survey of health care workers who are either infected or at risk of infection found, according to *The New York Times*, that "many infected health care workers have not told their patients or colleagues of their condition and continue to do invasive procedures" on unsuspecting patients. . . .

Too Great a Risk

The operating room and dentist's chair can be dangerous to your health. The Centers for Disease Control (CDC) estimates that over 7,000 health care workers contract hepatitis B virus each year from their patients and has documented 40 instances where physicians and nurses have contracted AIDS from their patients.

Patients, we now know, face their own concerns. Everyone knows of the tragic situation in Florida, where five patients of the late Dr. David Acer are infected. The CDC has calculated that as many as 128 patients have contracted AIDS from their health providers since 1981. Overall, CDC believes, there is an 8.1% chance that an HIV-infected surgeon will infect a patient. I think you will agree that these risks are simply too great for us to rely on the voluntary approach being championed by the AMA and its allies in the Congress.

II

Until recently there was no reason to believe that patients had any reason to fear contracting the AIDS virus from infected health-care workers. That is no longer the case. [Five] people in Florida, who tested positive for HIV (the human immunodeficiency virus, which causes AIDS), have been linked to a dentist who died of AIDS.

No one ever viewed HIV-infected health-care workers carrying out "invasive procedures" as a possible additional risk factor for the transmission of the AIDS virus. But it now seems evident that this should be considered a significant "risk."

Right to Know

So now the question becomes, do patients have the right to know whether their doctor or dentist is HIV-positive? And if so, who should tell them?

Moreover, should we insist on mandatory testing for health-care workers and should those who test positive for HIV or other blood-borne diseases (such as hepatitis B) be barred from doing invasive procedures (largely, those which involve contact with a patient's blood)?

Mandatory Testing Prevents HIV Infection

Our pilots and bus and train drivers have mandatory drug testing to protect the public against potential harm. Automobile drivers are subject to mandatory alcohol testing programs to protect innocent people from preventable harm, and our airports have mandatory antiterrorism systems in place which prevent well over 95% of terrorism acts from occurring. Mandatory testing for blood-borne diseases once a year and on random demand and linked to professional licensure would do the same to prevent HIV and hepatitis transmission in the vast majority of cases from health care workers to patients carrying out invasive procedures.

Sanford F. Kuvin, *Courts and the Law*, Summer 1991.

The Centers for Disease Control (CDC) will soon issue new guidelines for prevention of HIV transmission in health-care facilities. Some health professionals have raised concerns about restricting the duties of health-care workers. Others argue that there is insufficient evidence that HIV-infected workers pose a serious risk to patients.

Clearly, the patient has the right to know the risk of harm from a health-care provider, and vice versa. Decreasing this "risk" should be the key objective in formulating a new public health policy.

Thousands Infected

Currently, there are 156 dentists and 42 surgeons who have developed full-fledged AIDS. There are also thousands of additional health-care workers infected with HIV and chronic hepatitis B. The actual numbers of infected health-care workers is probably much higher, but we just don't know because of under-reporting, confidentiality and bureaucratic health practices.

In the Florida cases, investigators were able to link all [five] patients to the dentist with the help of sophisticated testing techniques. It marks the first time in the 10-year history of the AIDS epidemic that the transmission from an infected health-care worker to a patient has been documented.

It is reasonable to conclude that similar transmissions of HIV by health-care workers carrying out invasive procedures occurred long before the CDC guidelines were published in 1987 recommending "universal precautions" to prevent HIV and hepatitis B transmission in health-care settings. These precautions advise the use of gloves, masks, gowns and protective eye wear and consider "blood and certain bodily fluids of all patients potentially infectious for HIV, hepatitis B and other blood-borne pathogens."

However the risks to the patient with regard to HIV have yet to be addressed by the CDC.

This landmark case only came to the attention of the Centers for Disease Control because of the short (two-year) incubation period of the virus in one patient, Kimberly Bergalis, which allowed the blood of the dentist to be obtained for testing while the dentist was still alive. Had she fallen within the normal five- to eight-year incubation period before developing AIDS, the dentist would have long been dead, and there would be no blood available for testing.

Risks for Patients and Medical Workers

Health-care professionals also run a real risk of contracting HIV from patients. According to the American Medical Association, at least two dozen physicians become infected with the AIDS virus each year, usually without their ever remembering they came in contact with blood from an HIV-infected patient.

And another report found that 21 percent of medical students were stuck by HIV-contaminated needles during their third and fourth years of medical school.

Unfortunately universal precautions do not provide universal safety, and nothing in the guidelines refer to the risk of transmission from an HIV- or hepatitis B-infected health-care worker to a patient.

A Call for Routine Screening

The greatest risk factor for contracting HIV/AIDS for the general public is in the health care setting. We need laws in place that will benefit and protect everyone. Routine screening for HIV/AIDS for health care workers and patients entering the health care system is reasonable as well as affordable.

Norm Cadarette and Ginny Cadarette, *Manchester Union Leader*, September 2, 1991.

There are 150,000 dentists and about 500,000 physicians in the United States. Even if only 1 or 2 percent of infected health-care workers carry out invasive procedures that allow for the transmission of the virus, there will be many more Kimberly Bergalises. That is unconscionable and cannot be allowed to happen.

Setting Standards

We as health-care professionals must first act as role models in developing sound public health policy to protect the health of all Americans. We must do this in a *proactive* way, rather than in a *reactive* way, as has been the case. For instance:

• All health-care professionals involved in invasive procedures should have *mandatory* testing for HIV and chronic hepatitis B and make their status known to their patients. Testing should be linked to professional licensing requirements and the demands of liability insurers for malpractice coverage.

• Blood is a two-way street, and the patient undergoing invasive surgery must similarly be tested. Health-care workers also have a right to know.

• The Centers for Disease Control should issue new guidelines recommending that dentists and physicians who test positive for HIV not be allowed to perform any procedure in which they could come in contact with patients' blood.

• HIV reporting should be obligatory in all 50 states and jurisdictions to comply with the necessity to not only report HIV, but also to trace sexual partners, intervene with life-prolonging therapy and to guide pediatric and social-support programs.

Confidentiality can and must be maintained.

• From a medical, ethical and public health interest, state health officials should immediately summon for testing all patients of AIDS-infected health-care workers practicing invasive medicine and dentistry. (The AMA and the American Dental Association have said that dentists and surgeons infected with HIV have a voluntary ethical obligation to tell patients. That does not go far enough.)

• Significant programs must be enacted to ensure the economic safety of occupationally related HIV or hepatitis B injury to medical and dental students, residents, house staff and health-care workers with regard to workers' compensation, disability payments, life-insurance programs and alternative job placement and retraining programs.

• Legislation at the state and federal level, as well as regulation by the Occupational Safety and Health Administration must protect health-care providers *and* patients against the risk of blood-borne pathogens.

A central principle of medical ethics is "First, do no harm." How can a physician or dentist know that he or she will do no harm when he or she is a carrier of HIV, hepatitis B or any other blood-borne disease?

"Mandatory HIV testing of health care providers . . . would kill more people than [it] could possibly save."

Health Care Workers Should Not Be Tested for HIV

Evan Wolfson and Otis Damslet

Mandatory testing of health care workers would be ineffective at controlling the spread of AIDS, according to Evan Wolfson and Otis Damslet. In the following viewpoint, the authors maintain that proper infection control procedures prevent the spread of AIDS in the health care setting. They maintain that HIV transmission from health care workers is remote and that mandatory testing would unnecessarily increase health care costs. Wolfson is an attorney for Lambda Legal Defense, a lesbian and gay rights advocacy group. Damslet is a student at New York Law School.

As you read, consider the following questions:

1. Why do Wolfson and Damslet oppose forcing health care workers to reveal their HIV status?
2. Why do the authors maintain that mandatory testing will cause illegal discrimination of HIV-infected medical personnel?
3. How is the public miseducated about the spread of AIDS in the health care setting, according to the authors?

Evan Wolfson and Otis Damslet, "Gay Rights Advocates Speak Out," *Employment Testing* 5 (1 September 1991): BWR: 823, 830-31. Reprinted with the permission of University Publications of America.

Lambda Legal Defense and Education Fund regrets the decision of the Centers for Disease Control (CDC) to mix science with politics in their July 1991 guidelines on the human immunodeficiency virus (HIV) and infection control. On the one hand, we are pleased that the CDC emphasized the importance of universal precautions to prevent HIV transmission, the absence of any basis to recommend special restrictions on HIV-positive health care providers who perform invasive procedures not identified as "exposure-prone," and the fact that this vast majority of health care providers "pose[s] no risk" of HIV transmission. Lambda also concurs with the CDC's statement that "mandatory testing of HCWs [health care workers] . . . is not recommended." On the other hand, we condemn the CDC's political decision to suggest that health care providers performing that small set of "exposure-prone" procedures could be selectively forced to disclose their HIV status to prospective patients. That was politics, not public health, as evidenced by the last-minute shredding of thousands of issues of the *Morbidity and Mortality Weekly Report* to allow for the insertion, at the prompting of a Republican senator, of the provision on forced disclosure not reviewed by other public health experts.

Testing Does Not Help

Like the significant public health experts in this country, Lambda strongly opposes mandatory HIV testing of health care providers or any attempt to restrict them on the basis of their HIV status. Measures that penalize health care providers for being HIV positive illegally discriminate, needlessly provoke public panic, critically undermine the essential protective policies of universal precautions and infection control, and seriously damage the entire health care system.

Following the CDC's politicized mishandling of the Florida dentist case and the ensuing media sensationalism, the nation is in the midst of a resurgent AIDS hysteria. The last time the AFRAIDS (Acute Fear Regarding AIDS) epidemic reached such heights was in 1985, focusing on the issue of HIV-positive children in public schools. Teachers were fired, students were expelled, and some even had their homes firebombed before the panic subsided and reason returned. It is time now to quell the hysteria surrounding HIV-positive health care providers by looking at the facts.

FACT ONE: The risk of HIV transmission from health care providers to patients during even the most invasive procedures is extremely remote; patients are more likely to be killed by an asteroid than to contract the HIV from an HIV-positive health care provider.

In the millions of invasive procedures performed by HIV-positive health care providers since the HIV was discovered, there has never once been a single confirmed case of provider-to-patient HIV transmission. The CDC has reported that the only health care provider ever suspected of causing patients to become infected, Florida dentist David Acer, routinely ignored infection control procedures; there is no known case of provider-to-patient transmission when proper infection control was practiced. The CDC's investigation strongly suggests that the transmission in that office may have occurred from patient to patient through improperly sterilized equipment; Dr. Acer was in fact a patient in his own office. Patient-to-patient transmission reinforces the argument in favor of universal precautions and against testing health care providers. Universal precautions and infection control would have protected against patient-to-patient transmission; testing providers and forcing them to disclose their HIV status would not.

Health Care Workers Should Be Applauded

Public hysteria is pushing gay dentists and other health-care workers into the closet, whether they are HIV positive or not. The fact is, health-care workers are more at risk of receiving the virus than passing it on. They should be applauded for their work—not punished. Testing of health-care workers is a bad idea. The cost—estimated as high as $1.5 billion annually—would be better spent on education and care. The virus can exist in the body up to six months before registering on a test. Infected workers could test negative. Finally, the very act of testing makes the infinitesimal risks posed by infected workers seem far greater than they actually are.

Tom Ehrenfeld, *Newsweek*, October 14, 1991.

The health care setting abounds with risks that are more likely to occur than HIV transmission, but these hazards are routinely and properly ignored as too remote to be significant. A patient's risk of contracting the HIV is no greater than that same patient's risk of being killed in a car crash on the way to the hospital. There is no such thing as a risk-free environment, but with strong infection control, the health care setting can be made safe.

Infection Control Instead of Discrimination

FACT TWO: If they really want to make health care facilities safe, states should concentrate on the rigorous implementation and monitoring of universal precautions and infection control practices. All health care providers who are qualified to perform their jobs and who adhere to good standard infection control should continue their duties without special restrictions or conditions, including the forced disclosure of their HIV status. Universal precautions best protect both patients and health care providers from transmission of the HIV and all other infections; therefore what is needed is more monitoring of across-the-board infection control. Health care institutions should concentrate on cleaning up the workplace, rather than cleaning out needed workers.

FACT THREE: Forced disclosure of HIV status and widespread testing of health care providers would illegally discriminate against health care providers living with the HIV. Holding HIV-positive health care providers to a unique standard of disclosure would drive them from the profession without any benefit to the public, since the risk of transmission is infinitesimal and avoidable with basic infection control.

Federal law prohibits institutions receiving federal funds, including hospitals, from discriminating against employees on the basis of physical handicap unless the employees pose a significant risk to others. HIV-positive health care providers do not pose a significant risk to others; barring them from working with patients who do not know their HIV status would illegally and needlessly discriminate against them.

Even if there were a significant risk, the law requires employers to make reasonable efforts to accommodate those who have disabilities while reducing the risk. Universal precautions are a reasonable accommodation that virtually eliminates any chance of HIV transmission from health care providers to patients.

An Impossible Burden

FACT FOUR: Forced disclosure of health care providers' HIV status would constitute a radical and counterproductive departure from established informed consent law, which has never required the disclosure of risks as minuscule as the possibility of HIV transmission.

Requiring health care providers to explain every conceivable risk of every procedure would place an impossible burden on practitioners and provide no real benefit to patients. Accordingly, the courts and medical authorities have consistently rejected applying informed consent law to risks much greater than the tiny chance of HIV transmission. Transmission of hepatitis B, for example, is a much greater risk in the hospital setting, yet patients are not informed of that degree of risk. Studies of individual surgeons' performance in similar situations show that some are ten times more likely than others to cause potentially fatal postoperative infections in patients, yet patients are not informed of their individual doctors' postoperative wound infection rates. As many as 2 percent of practicing physicians suffer from recognized drug addictions, yet medical associations have always opposed disclosure of doctors' drug histories. The CDC should have rejected political pressure and condemned efforts to single out for intrusive disclosure the virtually nonexistent possibility of HIV transmission.

Virtually No Risk

FACT FIVE: The CDC guidelines expressly reject mandatory testing. Therefore, there is no basis for hospitals or insurers to require testing of health care providers.

Forcing HIV-positive health care providers to disclose their HIV status would drive many of them out of the profession, despite the fact that when they follow standard infection control procedures, they present virtually no risk to patients. The senseless loss to society of their valuable services would exacerbate already critical shortages of health care providers.

Knowledge Not Fear

The HIV screening of health professionals will not contribute much to a patient's safety. Worse, it will send the wrong message—that HIV-infected individuals are highly contagious and should be banished from the health care system.

With one million Americans HIV-positive, and those infected living longer, the chance that a surgeon's scalpel or dentist's drill have been used on an HIV-infected person is increasing. If sloppy techniques spread this virus, medicine has established ways to deal with the problem.

Until we do the research to accurately assess the risk of transmission from health professionals, we should move very carefully. The measures we take should be based on knowledge, not fear.

David E. Rogers and Bruce G. Gellin, *The New York Times*, July 16, 1991.

Requiring the disclosure of HIV status would radically change the standard of care in informed consent law. It would breed additional costly litigation in cases regarding other risks that are far greater than the risk of HIV transmission but normally considered too remote to merit disclosure. Plaintiffs' lawyers will argue that these remote risks affecting their clients should have been disclosed. Doctors and hospitals will then be forced to take part in more lawsuits, to pay more judgments and settlements, and to incur higher insurance premiums. If they try to institute forced testing to cover themselves against liability, they will be in violation of the law and will be sued. All these costs will ultimately be borne by patients.

The costs to the health care system of mandatory testing would also be enormous. It has been estimated that for a single hospital, periodic mandatory testing and resultant restrictions would cost more than $860,000 for the first year alone, more than twice that hospital's entire budget for infection control. The costs of testing, periodic retesting, enforcement, reallocation, and retraining could bankrupt many hospitals that are already financially strapped. The loss of hospitals would combine with the loss of health care providers and with increased costs to force health care prices up, thus denying access to additional millions of Americans who will be unable to afford health care or insurance.

Fatally Miseducating the Public

By inciting public fear over the near-zero risk of HIV transmission during health care, the media, medical trade guilds, and the CDC are fatally miseducating the public. Instead of worrying about illusory "killer hospitals," our political leaders should be sponsoring universal and targeted educational programs to teach people how the HIV is really spread on a daily basis. Instead of squandering millions of dollars arguing about this infinitesimal aspect of the HIV epidemic, our society should be focusing on preventing transmission where it really does occur. Instead of punishing health care providers for being HIV positive, we should be developing new treatments and programs to improve access to health care for all. Instead of wasting time and money fighting over phantoms, we should be finding a cure.

In conclusion, good public health in this country depends on our making policy on the basis of reason, not on the basis of fear or prejudice. The risk of HIV transmission from health care provider to patient is extremely remote and is best eliminated through the use of universal precautions. Mandatory testing programs or efforts to restrict HIV-positive health care providers would decrease the supply of health care and increase its cost, depriving millions of Americans of needed care. By reducing access to health care and driving skilled providers away from their lifesaving practices, policies like mandatory HIV testing of health care providers and forced disclosure of HIV status would kill more people than they could possibly save.

"Contact tracing . . . is one of the most important traditional methods for the control of disease transmitted primarily through sexual intercourse."

Contact Tracing Would Help Control AIDS

Ralph Dittman

In contact tracing, the sexual partners of patients infected with HIV are found and notified of their risk for developing the disease. According to Ralph Dittman in the following viewpoint, it is an effective way of preventing the spread of AIDS. Dittman argues that contact tracing eliminates disease and is inexpensive. He calls for national public health legislation requiring contact tracing for anyone found to be HIV positive. Dittman is a physician living in Houston, Texas.

As you read, consider the following questions:

1. How can contact tracing stop the spread of AIDS, according to Dittman?
2. Why does the author believe that confidentiality and discrimination will not be a problem in contact tracing?
3. Why was the Colorado contact tracing program a success, according to Dittman?

Adapted from Ralph Dittman, "AIDS Contact Tracing Controls Sexually Transmitted Diseases," *Saturday Evening Post*, May/June 1992. Reprinted with permission.

As of February 29th, 1992, the CDC reported 213,641 United States cases of AIDS. The CDC defines AIDS as a life-threatening manifestation of infection with the human immuno-deficiency virus (HIV). HIV gradually incapacitates the body's immune system, leaving the infected individual vulnerable to a wide variety of serious opportunistic infections and certain types of cancer. These infections and cancers are rare or only produce mild illness in individuals with normally functioning immune systems.

AIDS is a sexually transmitted disease. Today, it is an invariably fatal disease; the majority of AIDS patients die within two years of diagnosis. These two characteristics of AIDS factor into discussions of appropriate infection control measures. . . .

Partner Notification

Contact tracing, more aptly called "partner notification," is one of the most important traditional methods for the control of disease transmitted primarily through sexual intercourse. The tracing and notification of contacts for sexually-transmissible diseases (STDs) was originally proposed in the United States as part of the Chamberlain Kahn Act of 1918. The method was implemented as policy in 1937, under the guidance of Surgeon General Thomas Parran. Parran's popular book, *Shadow on the Land* (1937), assisted the passage of the LaFollette-Bulwinkle Bill of 1938, which set up a control program for syphilis and other diseases known to be sexually transmitted. The known STDs then included: gonorrhea, chancroid, lymphogranuloma venereum, and granuloma inguinale. Today STDs also include AIDS, chlamydia, hepatitis B, certain enteric infections, and possibly cervical cancer. Central to the prevention and control of syphilis was the early identification, notification and treatment of sexual contacts directly exposed to the disease through recent sexual contact. These contacts were at the greatest risk of development and spread of the disease. Thus, the expanding chains of syphilis transmission within a community could be broken.

Limited Attention

Contact tracing has also been employed to control diseases other than STDs which are directly transmitted from person-to-person by droplet spread or casual contact. Prior to modern effective methods of treatment, tuberculosis, a communicable disease, was largely controlled through early identification and isolation of infectious persons. The current resurgence of a drug-resistant strain of tuberculosis may reactivate these containment measures.

Only by intensive house-to-house searches for individuals exposed to smallpox cases were the last local foci of smallpox infection eliminated in May 1980 by the World Health Organization's global efforts (almost 200 years after an effective means of prevention became available). Where mass education, mass vaccination, and official reporting programs failed, active case-finding and contact tracing succeeded in finally eradicating this deadly disease.

Contact Tracing Can Be Useful

The Public Health Service believes that now that we have treatment for AIDS—in the sense that we can slow the progress of the disease—that there should be contact tracing. But the infected person must voluntarily agree to participate in this. Otherwise the tracing will not work in terms of preventing new infection. Confidentiality is essential. Contact tracing done professionally and with sensitivity can be a very useful measure in preventing future transmission of AIDS.

Antonia C. Novello, *Priorities*, Winter 1991.

When reliable HIV antibody tests became available in 1985, routine contact tracing for the control of HIV infection became possible. Though widely accepted for the control of other STDs, contact tracing has received only limited attention as a control measure for HIV. The length of the incubation period for AIDS, and the stage at which a case becomes infectious, is uncertain. However, it is a scientific fact that the disease can be transmitted to others long before the full-blown syndrome develops.

Legal and Moral Questions

AIDS is officially a reportable disease in all 50 states. HIV seropositivity is now reportable in 36 states, including the District of Columbia. Of this latter group, however, less than a third of those states require names to be reported and only 19 require notification of a spouse. As well, 29 states allow some variant of partner notification. Health department programs for contact tracing/partner notification for AIDS tend to be of three types: (1) health department personnel assist HIV-infected individuals who request that their past sexual partners be notified; (2) aggressive tracing of all contacts of all reported individuals with HIV infection; and (3) targeted contact tracing of specific populations such as women of childbearing age or partners of individuals exposed through blood transfusions. The lack of standard methods for HIV prevention and control by the 50 states raise major questions not only regarding the effectiveness and the legality, but issues of ethics and morality.

The issues of confidentiality and discrimination are complex and intertwined with the issues of mandatory testing, reportability, and partner notification. Hopefully, the Bush Administration's announcement that discrimination against AIDS cases will no longer be tolerated may remove one argument against contact tracing where confidentiality of data is assured by health professionals.

Must the rights of the individual always be protected at any risk to society? Do not individuals directly exposed to great danger have a right to know? In a democracy such as ours, the rights of individuals derive from the "social contract" that binds us together as a nation, a state, or a community. In times of great danger, for protection of the community, should not individuals give up a few rights?

These questions were posed by society long before the HIV epidemic. Historically, we have favored the majority. Quarantine regulations, contact tracing, and mandatory immunizations and testing (with or without informed consent) have been used to protect the public health. However, in the HIV epidemic issues of confidentiality and discrimination present very fundamental challenges to our society, particularly to the public health and legal systems.

Two Studies

One of the first studies of the cost-effectiveness of tracing of HIV cases was reported in the *Journal of the American Medical Association* (JAMA) in 1988. From one HIV antibody-positive man and his 19 reported sex contacts, a rural South Carolina health department identified 83 sex contacts of HIV antibody-positive men. Of those, 65 were residents of the county. Ninety-eight percent agreed to be tested for evidence of HIV infection. Thirteen percent were HIV antibody positive. Thirty-six initially HIV antibody-negative men were reevaluated at a six-month follow-up visit, and three had seroconverted during that time. Comparing reported numbers of sexual contacts for the six-month periods before and after their initial investigation, the mean numbers of named sex contacts decreased by 82% for antibody-positive men and 54% for antibody-negative men. None of the men reported using condoms before entering the study. At the six-month follow-up visit, 80% of the antibody-positive men and 69% of the antibody-negative men reported using condoms. The cost of the entire investigation, including salaries, benefits, and travel for field researchers and counselors, as well as HIV screening and western blot confirmation came to $100 cost-per-contact tested or $810 cost-per-HIV antibody-positive man identified.

An editorial in the same issue of *JAMA* thought it would be appropriate to concentrate resources on education. Not considered in the editorial was the fact that one-on-one education of sexual contacts may be much more effective in controlling this epidemic than mass education or mass screening.

The results of a contact tracing program at the Colorado Department of Health (*JAMA* 1988) were very similar to the South Carolina experience—a 13% antibody positive rate in sex contacts with the observation that "there is a return of at least $5 for every dollar invested in partner notification." The Colorado contact tracing/partner notification program was considered a major success for several reasons: "(1) a large number of partners were located and counselled; (2) individuals not previously diagnosed were found to be infected; (3) the intervention benefited various target groups who had not previously been influenced by general educational messages about safer sex; and (4) the cost was paltry, especially compared with the savings to be realized if only one case of AIDS was prevented by intervention."

National Effort

Federally directed health care leadership is desperately needed to coordinate a national or global battle against HIV. We need public health legislation not only to coordinate control and containment, but to prevent HIV discrimination, coordinate testing and reportability, and, generally, to spearhead a nationally concerted effort to prevent the spread of HIV from the 1 to 1.5 million citizens already infected. Where is today's urgently needed Thomas Parran?

> "We can 'protect' far more humanely . . . through education than through . . . contact tracing."

Contact Tracing Would Not Help Control AIDS

Glenn C. Graber and Caroline R. Graber

Mandatory contact tracing would not help control the spread of AIDS, Glenn C. Graber and Caroline R. Graber argue in the following viewpoint. The authors advocate voluntary testing and education as a way to stop the spread of HIV infection. Mandatory contact tracing would only inhibit individuals from getting tested, according to the authors. Glenn C. Graber is a professor of philosophy and medicine at the University of Tennessee at Knoxville. Caroline R. Graber is a registered nurse and works as an infection control/employee health coordinator in Knoxville.

As you read, consider the following questions:

1. What do the authors mean when they say HIV is not "inevitably fatal"?
2. How do the authors compare driving an automobile to the risk of getting AIDS?
3. What is the difference between a moral and a legal duty to notify past partners, according to the authors?

Adapted from Glenn C. Graber and Caroline R. Graber, "Mandatory Contact Tracing: An Idea Whose Time Should Never Come," a position paper expressly written for inclusion in the present volume.

A new sexually transmitted disease has arisen—Acquired Immunodeficiency Syndrome (AIDS), which is caused by the human immunodeficiency virus (HIV). It is perhaps more appropriate to speak of "HIV disease" instead of AIDS as the disease in question, in order to stress the continuity between infection by the virus and development of the immune system suppression that gives rise to the infections which define full-blown AIDS. We shall follow this usage. HIV disease is a devastating affliction. It is too strong to say that the disease is *inevitably* fatal. Some people who register HIV-positive have survived for many years without progressing to full-blown AIDS, and other HIV-positive people have experienced one or a few episodes of the infections that characterize AIDS and yet have remained free from further complications of the disease for many years. Drugs are now available—notably AZT—which appear to be fairly effective in slowing the progression of the disease. It is most accurate to say, then, that HIV disease is treatable, but not at present curable. Even those who do not progress on to AIDS remain HIV-positive and thus remain infectious.

Harm and Risk

The specter of HIV infection has led to a strong counterreaction. Some have proposed mandatory testing for HIV for a variety of categories of people and for strong protection measures to be taken against those who test HIV-positive, including mandatory tracing and notification of all with whom they have had intimate contact. In our judgment, however, such a policy would be unworkable, ineffective in controlling the HIV epidemic, and fraught with serious moral and legal injustices. . . .

Surely everyone would agree that, in general, one has a moral obligation not to cause harm to others. . . .

But it would be far too strong to generalize from this and say that one has a duty to refrain from *any and all* behavior with a *potential* to cause harm. A principle this strong would prohibit anyone from ever driving automobiles, for example, since (a) the emissions from auto exhaust cause some harm to the environment and some risk to the health of those with respiratory problems and (b) every time one goes onto the highway there is *some* chance of an accident that is fatal to another person.

Reaction to Risk

The appropriate reaction to risk includes these steps:

1) We all ought to be aware of the element of risk in everything we do, and we ought to include an assessment of these risks as a key component of our decisions about what to do. We might, for example, set a threshold of reasonable risk beyond which we would refuse to take part in an activity. (*For example,*

I might feel comfortable driving a car but decide that a motorcycle is too risky for me.)

2) We ought to take reasonable precautions to minimize the risk (*e.g., by wearing seat belts when we go out in an automobile, by driving sensibly, etc.*).

3) We ought to be especially conservative in the level of risk that we impose on others. We have a special responsibility to protect others, but this does not extend to protecting them from *all* risk. Furthermore, in some cases, the other party can be said to have actively *accepted* some degree of risk. For example, another driver who has ventured onto the highway should know of the possibility of fatal accident and thus can be said to have accepted a reasonable level of risk. The same cannot be said of children playing in their front yards, however, and thus we must be especially cautious towards them.

Appropriate Risks

There is *no* justification to bar HIV-infected persons from the schoolroom or the workplace. To be sure, there is *some* chance in these cases of an accident that would infect others, but the chance is so slight that it would be unreasonable to deprive these individuals of the opportunity to learn and work in order to guard others against infection. Precautions to minimize the risk are certainly appropriate (*i.e., what have come to be called "universal precautions"—ways of handling nosebleeds and other bodily fluids as if all were infectious*), but to bar people who are HIV-positive from these settings altogether seems to be a grossly exaggerated overreaction to the magnitude of the risk. . . .

Contact Tracing Is Ineffective

Advocates of reporting and contact tracing often cite the use of such programs in the control of gonorrhea and syphilis. However, gonorrhea and syphilis are far more contagious than is HIV; in other words, the probability of transmission of HIV in a single sexual contact is far lower. This has a dramatic effect on the value of contact tracing. Past attempts to employ contact tracing for hepatitis B, whose epidemiology is very similar to HIV, failed.

Robert M. Anderson and John M. Quigley, *The New York Times*, June 21, 1989.

What about sexual relations? Must we say to an adolescent who has been infected with HIV (perhaps through a blood transfusion or by means of his hemophilia treatment) that he must plan to abstain from sexual relations of all types throughout his life? We know of "safer" sex techniques which reduce the risk somewhat; but these do not entirely remove the risk of transmission of HIV to the sexual partner and, in fact, it is unlikely that they bring it within the limits of the risk threshold most people would find acceptable. One study estimates the risk of infection from one sexual encounter using a condom with a partner who is HIV-positive as 1 in 5,000; and the risk of infection from 500 sexual encounters as 1 in 11.

A time-honored reaction to risk in general has been to recognize a "duty to warn." If it would be too onerous to expect one to *remove* some hazard entirely, they can be expected at least to warn others of its presence. Applying this principle, we might hold that a person infected with HIV has a moral duty to warn prospective sexual partners of his or her condition and thereby allow them to make an informed decision about whether (a) to accept the risk, (b) to take steps to minimize the risk, or (c) to avoid the risky behavior entirely. . . .

Mandatory Contact Tracing

We acknowledged above that an HIV-positive individual has a moral duty to warn prospective sexual partners of their HIV status. However, a *moral* duty to warn *prospective* partners is a far cry from a *legal* policy *requiring* notification of *past* intimate contacts.

One question the latter raises is whether the *moral* duty should be sanctioned by *law*. Not every moral duty is a plausible candidate for legal enforcement. Among other things, we must consider the "costs" of legal enforcement in terms of invasion of privacy and violation of other important values, and we must determine whether adding legal enforcement brings sufficient benefit to justify these costs.

One technique that has been developed in the effort to control other venereal diseases has been to trace the intimate contacts of an infected person and then to treat these people as well as the initial patient. However, the justification for such action in these cases is that we can offer a definitive *cure* of the disease with which these people are infected. Usually the cure consists of a single injection, and thus the interference with their lifeplans is short-term and fairly minimal. However, we have no cure to offer to HIV-infected persons. All we can do is to remind them of the information about modes of HIV transmission that is being presented to the general public in myriad ways already.

Inefficient Method

Furthermore, it is not clear what is to be gained by making such tracing for HIV contacts legally "mandatory." We can mandate that public health workers *ask* those who test positive for the virus to name their intimate contacts; but the effectiveness of this request depends on the voluntary cooperation of the infected person. If they choose to withhold the names of some contacts—or if they choose to harass someone by naming them falsely as an intimate contact—there is little we can do in response. Aggressive detective work might reveal some additional information; but this would be expensive, time-consuming and intrusive on the civil liberties of a wide circle of associates and acquaintances of the infected individual. And, even then, it is unlikely to be 100% effective. Discreet encounters might never be discovered.

Transmission through needle-sharing is even less likely to be eradicable by this means. How likely is it that people will know the names of all those with whom one has shared needles? They may have no way of knowing all who had used a given needle before it was offered to them, and there apparently are fairly large-scale and somewhat impersonal gatherings of people who pass around syringes in a communal drug experience.

The Problems of Contact Tracing

Opponents of tracing sex partners argue that it has failed to eradicate venereal disease. A New York City study showed that people often withhold names when asked to identify partners. . . .

Some who question the effectiveness of tracing partners for AIDS note the long lag from infection to symptoms, and the anonymity and multiplicity of drug and sex partners. Dr. Larry Gostin of Harvard said, "In the New York or San Francisco gay community, it's almost an exercise in futility." Health experts recommend that every drug user who has shared needles and every man who has had intercourse with another man should assume they may be infected and consider being tested.

Bruce Lambert, *The New York Times*, May 13, 1990.

Research suggests that the length of incubation may be months to years. How far back into a person's sexual history and/or drug-use history would we have to go to be effective in identifying all whom they may have infected? Furthermore, even when we reach those who have been exposed to the virus, we have no legal authority to mandate any specific behavioral response on their part. We cannot at present mandate that they be tested for HIV infection. And, if we could and they turn out to be HIV-positive, the only way to *remove* the threat they pose to others in a way parallel to offering the definitive treatment of syphilis would be to quarantine them for the remainder of their lives.

We must also consider the long-term effects of such a policy. It will soon become known that this sort of "harassment" is going on; and people who suspect that they are infected will be less inclined to come in for testing. This, in turn, may undercut the voluntary restraints in behavior that can make a difference in the spread of the disease.

Far more appropriate than ineffective legal approaches like mandatory contact tracing would be an intensive educational effort to make everyone aware of (a) the behaviors that put one at risk for acquiring and transmitting the disease and (b) the precautions that can be taken to minimize this risk. There is evidence that patterns of sexual behavior are changing—especially in the male homosexual community, but also among teenagers and young singles. Regrettably, this change is not as rapid or as complete as we would like, but it offers some basis for hope. The IV drug using population is more resistant to change, but redoubled efforts at education combined with syringe-exchange programs may be more effective in the long run than a punitive program of mandatory contact tracing.

The effectiveness of these programs can be enhanced still further if we work to remove the stigma of HIV-infection. As long as people are at risk of losing their jobs, being evicted from their housing, and being harassed by friends and strangers when they are detected to be HIV-positive, they will be reluctant to undergo testing to determine if they are HIV-positive. And not knowing may delay them from initiating voluntary lifestyle changes and notification of past sexual and needle-sharing partners.

A Question of Values

The HIV epidemic calls us as a society to a fundamental value choice: are we going to be a society of people who are fearful, suspicious, and exclusionary—who associate this health threat as a problem of "them" against "us" and take action to label and regiment those identified as infected? Or, in contrast, are we to recognize that "we are all in this together"—i.e., that this is a health problem that involves our neighbors, co-workers, friends, and family and which we must address in a humane and caring way?

We can "protect" far more humanely—and, we are convinced, more effectively in the long run—through education than through mandatory screening and contact tracing.

"It is time for routine testing of infants at risk for HIV, with or without parental consent."

Mandatory Testing of High-Risk Infants Is Necessary

Barbara Ruhe Grumet

Infants at risk of having contracted AIDS should be tested with or without parental consent, according to Barbara Ruhe Grumet. In the following viewpoint, Grumet maintains that if a doctor knows that a fetus or baby is HIV positive, illnesses and infections would be treated differently than in a non-infected fetus or infant. She contends that the child's welfare overrides the parents' privacy. Grumet is a political science and public administration professor at Sage College graduate school in Albany, New York.

As you read, consider the following questions:

1. What challenges need to be addressed in order to establish mandatory testing, according to the author?
2. Why does Grumet believe that testing high-risk infants is justified?
3. The author recommends following certain procedures before requiring high-risk infants to be tested. What are these procedures?

Over 4000 cases of pediatric AIDS have been reported to the Centers for Disease Control since the beginning of the AIDS epidemic. Virtually all cases reported since March 1985, when screening of the blood supply began, have been due to perinatal infection.

In spite of the fact that more infants are born with human immunodeficiency virus (HIV) infection than suffer from a variety of other conditions for which prenatal or newborn screening is routinely conducted (e.g., rubella, neural tube defects, and phenylketonuria [PKU]), experts still adhere to the "party line" that all testing for HIV should be done only after the subject has given voluntary, informed consent. However, these arguments do not justify the possible jeopardy to the newborn infant's health that failure to detect HIV status poses. New treatments for HIV and opportunistic infections, although not a cure, may delay the onset of AIDS and significantly improve the quality of life for infected infants. The benefits to the child outweigh any parental rights to withhold consent for testing for HIV. It is time for routine testing of infants at risk for HIV, with or without parental consent. . . .

Advantages of Testing for HIV

1. *Early detection of HIV will lead to better care for the infant.* Although there is currently no cure for HIV infection or AIDS, there are treatments that are routinely offered to individuals who have been exposed to HIV, regardless of whether they do indeed have the disease themselves. Zidovudine has been approved by the Food and Drug Administration for use in infants. Dideoxyinosine has been reported as effective in treating pediatric HIV. The Centers for Disease Control has issued guidelines for the prevention of *Pneumocystis carinii* pneumonia in infants. Although the drugs have their risks, they are substantially less than the risks of AIDS itself. Pediatricians report that if they knew that a child were HIV positive, they would treat other illnesses and infections more aggressively than they might otherwise. IVIG [an intravenous drug] therapy has been found to significantly improve the quality of life of children who are HIV positive or who have AIDS. An infant who has tested positive for HIV would also be monitored more carefully than other newborns might be. A final reason for knowing the newborn's HIV status is that, if new treatments become available, aggressive outreach could be used to locate and treat these infants.

2. *The traditional responsibility of the state to protect the best interest of the child justifies determining which infants are at risk for developing HIV and AIDS.* State laws have authorized medical care for children, regardless of parental wishes, because the child's need for care supersedes any parental rights to make de-

cisions on behalf of their children. In most states, care is authorized if the child's life or health would be seriously jeopardized by failure to provide the care. Surely, when a child may be at risk for a disease that is invariably fatal, the state has a significant interest in determining whether the child is at risk, in order to provide whatever treatment may be available. Even if a cure is not currently available, existing treatments may delay the onset of AIDS itself or significantly improve the quality of life for HIV-positive infants. However, these treatments cannot be provided unless the health care providers know that a newborn is at risk for HIV.

Testing High-Risk Individuals

Lingering social and political concerns over the consequences of mandatory testing of any group of patients probably render a call for routine testing of all pregnant women infeasible at the present time. Physicians should obviously continue to counsel high-risk pregnant women and encourage them to undergo voluntary testing. However, traditional medical, public health, and legal concerns for the health and well-being of children do support testing at least some infants for HIV, regardless of parental wishes or concerns for the consequences of the information obtained from such testing.

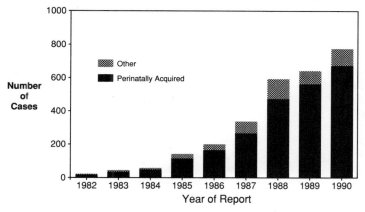

AIDS in Children (Less than 13 Years of Age)

Centers for Disease Control, *HIV/AIDS Prevention Newsletter*, Special Report, July 1991.

At the present time, there is probably not significant justification for routinely testing all 4 million newborn infants for HIV.

Such a massive undertaking would add substantially to the costs of medical care.

However, there are significant medical justifications for routinely testing certain categories of infants. Traditional public health approaches would justify testing at-risk individuals. These might include:

1. Infants born to women who are drug abusers

2. Infants born to women with a history of sexually transmitted diseases

3. Infants who are suffering symptoms of drug withdrawal shortly after birth

4. Infants born to women who are members of known risk categories

5. Infants with a sibling or parent who is HIV positive, or has AIDS, or has died from AIDS.

An alternative, given the social stigma and other consequences of such selective testing, would be to test all infants born in states or cities where the prevalence of HIV in the general population is greater than ten per 100,000. As of March 1991, 19 states, the District of Columbia, and the Commonwealth of Puerto Rico had a prevalence this high. By testing the newborns in these areas, virtually all the nation's HIV-positive infants will be detected.

Cannot Martyrize Children

Any testing program must include increased education, counseling, and treatment services for maternal drug abuse. It would be unconscionable to begin more widespread testing of infants for HIV without addressing the reality that testing the infant is, indeed, testing the mother. In addition, confidentiality and antidiscrimination protections must be enhanced, to deal with the widespread social consequences that knowledge of an individual's HIV status may produce.

Any testing of this sort involves a balancing of interests. The disadvantages and costs of testing must be weighed against the advantages and benefits. The latter are now strong enough to justify more routine testing of newborns.

Concerns for the mother's psychological and social well-being are not strong enough to sacrifice the child's possible future health. For decades, when children's interests and parents' interests conflict, courts have taken the posture that parents may be free to become martyrs themselves, but are not free to martyrize their children. During the early phases of the AIDS epidemic, when there were no known treatments, confidentiality and social concerns for the parent were stronger than any need to know the HIV status of the infant. Now, however, treatments are available that may prolong the child's life, improve the quality of life, and perhaps even forestall the onset of AIDS itself.

Ideally, newborns should be tested for HIV only after the voluntary, informed consent of the mother. However, the interests of determining which newborns are at significant risk for HIV are strong enough to justify testing without parental permission. Other serious conditions are tested for without parental consent. State legislatures should amend their public health laws to require testing of newborns if either the state's prevalence of HIV in the population, or the child's risk factors, warrant. The child's health and well-being should not be sacrificed to worries that the mother might suffer psychological or social consequences.

"Mandatory (involuntary) testing may not necessarily be the most effective way to ensure that the largest number of children are tested."

Mandatory Testing of High-Risk Infants Is Unnecessary

American Academy of Pediatrics Task Force on Pediatric AIDS

Mandatory testing of infants at a high risk for carrying the AIDS virus should not be required, according to the Task Force on Pediatric AIDS. In the following viewpoint, the task force contends that testing newborns is useless because not all newborns who test positive remain HIV positive. Mandatory tests may only stigmatize the parents and the child and provide no immediate medical benefit to the infants. The task force provides guidelines and recommendations for the care of infants, children, and adolescents with HIV infection and drafts American Academy of Pediatrics policy statements concerning these groups.

As you read, consider the following questions:

1. How do a majority of infants become infected with the AIDS virus, according to the authors?
2. Under what conditions do the authors approve of HIV testing for infants?
3. The authors are against mandatory testing because they contend that it would not prove that an infant would develop AIDS. What other arguments do the authors present against mandatory testing?

Adapted from "Perinatal Human Immunodeficiency (HIV) Testing," written by and used with permission of the American Academy of Pediatrics Task Force on Pediatric AIDS, 1992.

The primary route of HIV infection in infants is vertical transmission from HIV-infected mothers. This is of particular concern as the number of infected women and the number of children infected by perinatal transmission continue to increase rapidly. The number of perinatally acquired AIDS cases increased 17 percent in 1989 and 21 percent in 1990. Similarly, the number of heterosexually acquired AIDS cases increased 27 percent in 1989 and 40 percent in 1990. There is evidence that vertical transmission of HIV can occur in utero (congenital/ transplacental, similar to rubella), in the postpartum period (breast-feeding), and perhaps in the intrapartum period (similar to hepatitis B). The relative frequency and efficiency of transmission during each of these periods remains uncertain. The best estimates of vertical transmission from an HIV seropositive mother to the fetus range from 12.9 percent to 39 percent. Although the risk of transmission appears to be increased in women who are symptomatic, this point is still unclear. . . .

Seroprevalence

Anonymous seroprevalence data from newborn specimens are being collected in 44 states, Puerto Rico, and the District of Columbia. In some states, seroprevalence data are available by metropolitan area and/or by hospital of birth. Data from completed surveys are available from 38 states. The overall US seroprevalence rate from these studies is 1.5/1000 although there is at least a ten-fold geographic variation. Seroprevalence is highest in metropolitan areas, but it is increasing in small (50,000–100,000 population) urban and rural areas. It is important that anonymous seroprevalence testing be continued and expanded to monitor trends in maternal infection and estimates of future cases of pediatric HIV infections.

It should be noted that because the HIV antibody is passively transferred, testing of newborns provides only seroprevalence data for their mothers and does not prove infection of the newborn. New laboratory tests have been developed that may allow early (6 months of age) identification of HIV infection in young infants. . . .

Access to Care

To justify a successful perinatal HIV counseling and testing program, women and their families must have access to care, including developmental screening and care programs for newborns. However, counseling and testing programs that may benefit the mother, fetus, and newborn cannot be delayed until access problems have been completely resolved. Services must be provided for the families as well as for individual HIV-infected women and should include psychosocial, behavioral, and clinical support. Care systems based on case management are particularly suited for the care of the family and must include counseling before and after testing. Assessment and reduction of risks should be part of initial counseling; however, testing should be offered to all and not based solely on self-identified risk factors. Testing should be done only with pretest education, written informed consent, including the risks and benefits of testing for themselves and their infants, and post-test counseling on the meaning and implications of test results.

U.S. Pediatric AIDS Cases
Reported June 1990 Through May 1991

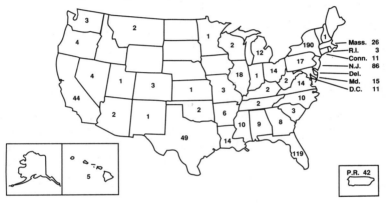

Mass.	26
R.I.	3
Conn.	11
N.J.	86
Del.	
Md.	15
D.C.	11

P.R. 42

Centers for Disease Control, *HIV/AIDS Prevention Newsletter*, Special Report, July 1991.

The costs of perinatal HIV testing include direct costs such as counseling, obtaining informed consent, testing, follow-up and managing HIV seropositive individuals, and indirect costs such as time and travel for those tested. There are other costs that are tangible although these are often difficult to quantify precisely. These costs include functional impairment due to psychologic distress while awaiting test results and after learning a test is positive, as well as adverse social consequences, including ostracism and loss of employment, with resulting loss of health insurance and other discrimination. Seropositive persons, including those who are false-positive, also experience adverse consequences associated with complications of medical treatment. Because of the extraordinary high specificity of the ELISA and Western Blot tests (>99.9 percent) the positive predictive value will be high (and negative predictive value low), even in low-prevalence areas.

The costs of identifying persons who are HIV seropositive are often compared to the savings associated with potentially reduced medical care expenses that may result with early intervention. In general, society is willing to pay for medical benefits, but not in excessive amounts, particularly when there are countless interventions of proven benefit for which resources could also be allocated. Therefore, it is customary to calculate the cost of achieving any specific outcome via cost-effectiveness analysis. Because both mother and infant benefit from perinatal HIV screening, costs for benefits to each need to be calculated according to documented efficacy (e.g., cost for prolonged time the infant is free of infection, cost of hospitalization averted, cost per episode of pneumonia averted, cost per case identified, and cost of averting a subsequent infant at risk for HIV infection). Cost-effectiveness analysis is an essential part of the ongoing evaluation of the effectiveness and appropriateness of any testing program. Currently, the limited data about the efficacy of early treatment of HIV infection and the magnitude of psychological and social costs that accompany testing makes meaningful cost-effectiveness analysis an extraordinary problem that may become easier as our information base improves.

Risks and Benefits

A newborn who is HIV seropositive has an HIV seropositive mother; therefore, testing newborns using existing methods constitutes indirect maternal testing. As such, some women may be deterred from seeking prenatal care.

If identification of affected infants is associated with treatment, such testing is indicated. Therefore, short- and long-term risks of treatment must be included in an assessment of risks of neonatal testing. This is of particular concern since at least two-thirds of those infants who are HIV seropositive will not be infected and may be exposed to risks of treatment that could possibly be harmful with no potential benefit.

Other risks of perinatal HIV testing are similar to those of identifying any other HIV-infected patients and are due primarily to parental anxiety and societal stigmatization.

The major medical benefits of perinatal testing and identification of HIV include a possible increase in life expectancy and better quality of life through the prevention, delay, or alleviation of HIV-related symptoms. Even when there are medical benefits for HIV-infected children, there may be other reasons to oppose mandatory testing. Mandatory (involuntary) testing may not necessarily be the most effective way to ensure that the largest number of children are tested. IVIG [an intravenous drug] has been shown to prolong the time of development of serious bacterial infection in HIV-infected children with CD4 (T4 helper) cell counts of greater than 200. Zidovudine has been shown to be beneficial in both adults and children. *Pneumocystis carinii* Pneumonia (PCP) prophylaxis using TMP/SMX or aerosol pentamidine has been shown to be beneficial for HIV-infected adults, and TMP/SMX is beneficial for children with leukemia. While the benefit of such prophylaxis in HIV-infected infants and children has not been demonstrated in a controlled trial, PCP in infants often presents fulminantly and has a high mortality rate, particularly in infants younger than 12 months. Therefore, guidelines have been developed and prophylaxis is recommended for children based on age adjusted CD4 cell counts. To summarize, the potential medical benefits to mothers and infected newborns include: 1) reduced morbidity due to intensive health and developmental supervision, including chemoprophylaxis, PCP prophylaxis, prophylaxis and early treatment of bacterial infections, and appropriate immunizations; 2) an opportunity for early antiretroviral therapy; 3) the provision of information regarding the risk of transmission from breast milk and the risk of vertical transmission in subsequent pregnancies; and 4) possible prevention of sexual transmission through education of the mother and father.

A Policy Against Mandatory Screening

A policy of mandatory screening either for pregnant women or for newborns is not justified in the current situation on traditional public health criteria or other grounds. Moreover, we reject implementation of counseling and screening policies that interfere with women's reproductive freedom or that result in the unfair stigmatization of vulnerable social groups.

Working Group on HIV Testing of Pregnant Women and Newborns, *Journal of the American Medical Association*, November 14, 1990.

The American Academy of Pediatrics believes that counseling and testing for HIV should be available to both men and women (regardless of a woman's pregnancy status) and should be recommended to many of these individuals. HIV antibody testing programs should be voluntary and accompanied by appropriate education, counseling, informed consent, and confidentiality. In addition, testing programs and policies should reflect cultural, ethnic, and community values. A newborn who is HIV seropositive has an HIV seropositive mother; therefore, testing newborns using existing methods constitutes indirect maternal testing.

The following recommendations specifically address the perinatal period:

1) HIV testing should be routinely offered to all pregnant women and women of childbearing age throughout the United States by informing them of availability of counseling and testing.

2) HIV testing should be routinely recommended and encouraged for all pregnant women and women of childbearing age at increased risk of HIV infection because of high-risk behaviors or because they live in areas (state, metropolitan area, city, etc) with an HIV seroprevalence rate among pregnant women and newborns of 1:1000 or more.

3) Newborn testing should be routinely recommended and encouraged when mothers with known high-risk behaviors or from high-seroprevalence areas have not been tested.

4) HIV testing should be recommended and encouraged for abandoned infants and for infants otherwise in need of foster or adoptive care as needed to facilitate placement and care. Courts should adopt methods for rapid processing of court orders to allow HIV testing of abandoned infants or those in foster care when follow-up adoption or initial placement may be facilitated by such testing.

5) Testing in the perinatal period should occur under specified policies which ensure retesting, education, informed consent, counseling, and follow-up criteria.

6) Anonymous seroprevalence surveys should be continued and expanded to identify hospital, city, and state seroprevalence information. These surveys are not a substitute for individual counseling and testing, but they provide important public health information.

7) Pilot studies of the benefits of perinatal testing, with careful evaluation of costs, are needed.

8) Specific tests for early diagnosis of HIV infection in infants must be further developed and made readily available to distinguish infection from passive transfer of maternal antibody.

9) Pediatricians or other primary pediatric care givers should be informed whenever an infant is born to a known HIV seropositive mother so that appropriate care and follow-up testing can be done.

10) It is inappropriate to develop testing programs without addressing access to care. However, testing programs that may benefit the mother, fetus, and newborn cannot be delayed until access problems have been completely resolved.

11) The American Academy of Pediatrics opposes mandatory (involuntary) maternal and/or newborn testing at this time.

a critical thinking activity

Evaluating Sources of Information

When historians study and interpret past events, they use two kinds of sources: primary and secondary. Primary sources are eyewitness accounts. For example, the speech of an AIDS researcher discussing the latest advances in finding a cure would be a primary source. A newsletter that prints the researcher's findings would be a secondary source. Primary and secondary sources may be decades or even hundreds of years old, and often historians find that the sources offer conflicting and contradictory information. To fully evaluate documents and assess their accuracy, historians analyze the credibility of the documents' authors and, in the case of secondary sources, analyze the credibility of the information the authors used.

Historians are not the only people who encounter conflicting information, however. Anyone who reads a daily newspaper, watches television, or just talks to different people will encounter many different views. Writers and speakers use sources of information to support their own statements. Thus, critical thinkers, just like historians, must question the writer's or speaker's sources of information as well as the writer or speaker.

While there are many criteria that can be applied to assess the accuracy of a primary or secondary source, for this activity you will be asked to apply three. For each source listed on the following page, ask yourself the following questions: First, did the person actually see or participate in the event he or she is reporting? This will help you determine the credibility of the information—an eyewitness to an event is an extremely valuable source. Second, does the person have a vested interest in the report? Assessing the person's social status, professional affiliations, nationality, and religious or political beliefs will be helpful in considering this question. By evaluating this you will be able to determine how objective the person's report may be. Third, how qualified is the author to be making the statements he or she is making? Consider what the person's profession is and how he or she might know about the event. Someone who has spent years being involved with or studying the issue may be able to offer more information than someone who simply is offering an uneducated opinion; for example, a politician or layperson.

Keeping the above criteria in mind, imagine you are writing a paper on whether the present methods used to control the spread of AIDS are adequate. You decide to cite an equal number of primary and secondary sources. Listed below are several sources that may be useful for your research. *Place a P next to those descriptions you believe are primary sources. Place an S next to those descriptions you believe are secondary sources.* Next, based on the above criteria, *rank the primary sources, assigning the number (1) to what appears to be the most valuable, (2) to the source likely to be the second-most valuable, and so on, until all the primary sources are ranked. Then rank the secondary sources, again using the above criteria.*

P or S

Rank in
Importance

_____ 1. The brochure *AIDS: The Alarming Reality*, _____ written by a doctor for a group called the Human Immunodeficiency Virus Eradication, a group calling for the quarantine of all AIDS patients.

_____ 2. Guidelines by the Centers for Disease _____ Control (CDC) that state what precautions dentists should use in their offices to prevent the spread of AIDS.

_____ 3. A commentary in a medical magazine about _____ the American Medical Association's statement on mandatory testing of health care workers.

_____ 4. A newspaper editorial in the *Los Angeles* _____ *Times* that says doctors should not practice if they have HIV.

_____ 5. A magazine article about an orthopedic sur- _____ geon who says that AIDS is spread by casual contact.

_____ 6. A book about gay rights that uses statements _____ from a brochure put out by the gay activist organization ACT UP.

_____ 7. A *New York Times* article that states that doc- _____ tors do not follow the U.S. guidelines to prevent AIDS.

_____ 8. A newspaper article about testing health _____ care workers that quotes a speech given before a congressional committee by a nurse with AIDS.

_____ 9. Viewpoint six in this chapter. [American _____ Academy of Pediatrics]

_____ 10. A New York newspaper that uses govern- _____ ment research to write a story about the medical procedures used to protect the public from AIDS.

Periodical Bibliography

The following articles have been selected to supplement the diverse views presented in this chapter.

Dennis L. Breo   "Meet Kimberly Bergalis — The Patient in the 'Dental AIDS Case'," *Journal of the American Medical Association*, October 17, 1990. Available from the American Medical Association, 515 N. State St., Chicago, IL 60610.

Richard L. Burke   "AIDS Battle Reverting to 'Us Against Them'," *The New York Times*, October 6, 1991.

Lindley H. Clark Jr.   "HIV Testing Bans Won't End 'Testing'," *The Wall Street Journal*, December 27, 1991.

Dennis de Leon and Alisa Lebow   "AIDS and Rape Suspects: A Smart Test?" *The New York Times*, June 1, 1991.

Michael Fumento   "Put to the Test," *Reason*, May 1992.

Barbara Kantrowitz et al.   "Doctors and AIDS," *Newsweek*, July 1, 1991.

Frank Morriss   "Kimberly Bergalis Was a Victim of Manslaughter," *Wanderer*, January 2, 1992. Available from 201 Ohio St., St. Paul, MN 55107.

National Review   "Private Grief," July 29, 1991.

New York Academy of Medicine   "The Risk of Contracting HIV Infection in the Course of Health Care," *Journal of the American Medical Association*, April 10, 1991.

Anna Quindlen   "No Bright Lines," *The New York Times*, July 7, 1991.

Second Opinion   "Health Care Workers, Patients, and HIV Infection," January 1992. Available from Park Ridge Center, 676 N. St. Clair, Suite 450, Chicago, IL 60611.

Sari Staver   "Physicians to Report Physicians?" *American Medical News*, November 11, 1991. Available from the American Medical News Association, 515 N. State St., Chicago, IL 60610.

Hilary Stout   "Grim Debate," *The Wall Street Journal*, April 22, 1992.

Anastasia Toufexis   "AIDS Moves in Many Ways," *Time*, June 3, 1991.

Elizabeth M. Whelan   "Rhetoric, Finger Pointing: Obstacles to Progress Against AIDS," *Priorities*, Fall 1990. Available from the American Council on Science and Health, 1995 Broadway, 16th Fl., New York, NY, 10023-5860.

How Can the Spread of AIDS Be Prevented?

Chapter Preface

AIDS should be a relatively simple disease to prevent. It is spread most commonly by sexual intercourse or by sharing needles while shooting drugs. The simplest prevention method would be to abstain from behaviors that spread HIV. However, this is more easily said than done, for changing human behavior and attitudes can be very difficult. AIDS experts favor two approaches to prevent AIDS. Each requires modifications in people's behavior.

One approach is to increase the safety of the behaviors that lead to the spread of HIV. This approach, many health experts and community activists maintain, accepts that people will continue to engage in dangerous behaviors such as promiscuous sex and intravenous drug use. Therefore, these people believe the only way to stop AIDS' spread is to distribute condoms and establish programs to teach students about safe sex. Many of these experts also recommend needle-exchange programs to help prevent AIDS among intravenous drug users. In support of these efforts, Rod Sorge, the needle-exchange program coordinator for ACT UP in New York, states:

> Many of our laws and cultural mores regarding sexuality (like prostitution and sodomy laws) and drug use (such as hypodermic possession and drug paraphernalia) only create a climate that promotes silence, secrecy, hate, and shame at a time when we need to be talking openly about sex and drug use. It is not surprising, then, that most of the AIDS prevention education that has been effective has been developed outside of government agencies and in the communities at which it is aimed.

Other experts, however, object to programs that accept AIDS-related behaviors and that attempt to make them "safe." Instead, they urge abstinence. They maintain that safe sex and needle-exchange programs are immoral because they promote drug use and premarital, extramarital, and homosexual sex. Abstinence, they argue, would effectively prevent the spread of the AIDS virus and at the same time restore moral values to the United States. Herbert Ratner, editor of *Child and Family Quarterly* supports this view. He states, "Perhaps if we put our energies to educating and persuading young people, boys and girls, men and women, to think 'no,' to say 'no,' and to act 'no,' we would get much further in curbing AIDS than by urging them to carry condoms in their purses and wallets."

Until there is a cure for AIDS, the debate over the best way to prevent it will continue. The viewpoints in the following chapter discuss various methods of preventing the spread of HIV infection.

"To prevent HIV infection, women have to insist that their partners use condoms."

Condom Use Will Help Prevent AIDS

Sara Nelson

Using condoms during sex can reduce the chance of one partner infecting the other with HIV, argues Sara Nelson. Nelson, a freelance writer and volunteer for an AIDS organization, charges that while many women are aware of the need to use condoms, they still believe they are unlikely to contract AIDS and therefore do not require that their male partners use them. People's attitudes about AIDS and condom use must change if AIDS is to be prevented, Nelson contends.

As you read, consider the following questions:

1. According to the author, why are people finding it so difficult to use condoms consistently?
2. What is the risk of AIDS to women, according to Nelson?
3. What does the author recommend to overcome women's resistance to insisting that men use condoms?

Adapted from Sara Nelson, "Talking Smart, Acting Stupid About AIDS," *Glamour*, February 1992. Reprinted with permission.

Whether you call it cognitive dissonance or denial, now, more than ten years into the AIDS epidemic, it seems that smart women are making foolish choices when it comes to AIDS prevention. "I always use condoms the first time with someone new," says one woman. "Sure, I keep condoms in the bedside drawer," says another, as if their mere presence is all that's required. A recent study confirms this dangerous dichotomy: *Knowing about safer sex and practicing it are all too often separate matters.* In a survey of 5,500 Canadian college students, researchers found that, despite high levels of AIDS awareness, fewer than 16 percent of the women studied said they always have their partner use condoms. Another study revealed that only one-fifth of the sexually active students at the University of Florida always use condoms during intercourse. More encouraging is a study suggesting that condom use among college students at one university increased from 12 percent in 1975 to 41 percent in 1989. Though that's a notable, heartening leap, it isn't the whole picture; a survey conducted during the 1988-1989 school year found that two in one thousand college students tested positive for HIV. A follow-up study conducted one year later showed similar results.

Women and AIDS

Why are so many savvy women not doing all they can to protect themselves from what is still an incurable disease? "Every group has its own reasons for not admitting AIDS risk," says Mindy Fullilove, M.D., of the HIV Center for Clinical and Behavioral Studies at Columbia University. "Women, for example, don't perceive themselves to be at risk. Even if they understand that there are dangerous behaviors, they haven't translated those dangers to themselves. Women use the fact that more men than women have gotten AIDS so far as an excuse. They say, 'I'm not at risk because AIDS is something men get.'"

What can explain this irrational response? "The idea of having to get a man to use a condom goes against everything that women have fought for," says Anke Ehrhardt, Ph.D., also of Columbia's HIV Center for Clinical and Behavioral Studies. "The development of the birth control pill made women more independent. But since condoms have to be worn by men, women have to depend on men to take action. Many aren't confident that men will take that responsibility, and they resent that a part of their sexuality—which they've fought so hard to embrace—is now in men's hands."

It's no wonder, then, that the whole issue of AIDS prevention has unleashed some powerful anger between the sexes. "I'd been dating a guy for a couple of weeks," says Nancy, a twenty-eight-year-old lawyer. "We hadn't slept together yet, but it was going in that direction. We'd gone to see *Pretty Woman*, and you know that scene where she pulls out a bunch of brightly colored condoms? I said something afterward about how they looked so silly, but it was good that movies were now addressing the issue of AIDS and condoms. I thought this was kind of an unthreatening, impersonal way to broach the subject. You know what the guy did? He laughed and said, 'Yeah, but she was a *hooker*. You've never been a hooker, have you?' I felt completely dismissed, that he wasn't taking the subject or me seriously—that if I insisted he use a condom, I'd be saying that I was some kind of slut."

Condoms Reduce Risk

Latex condoms—not the lambskin variety—used during vaginal, oral or anal sex substantially reduce risk.

Too few teens heed the safe-sex message. About 30% have sex by age 15, 70% by 18. Two-thirds of sexually active boys don't always use condoms.

AIDS risk may be small for some. But condoms still make sense.

USA Today, February 19, 1992.

Having a woman introduce the idea of using a condom does bring out the Neanderthal in some men. "I know I'm not supposed to feel that it's weird when a woman reveals that she carries them around with her," says Bob, twenty-eight, "but, well, it makes me think she's the kind of person who has sex on the run. I've had that kind of encounter, but it's not an encounter I'm proud of. Besides, it still feels different to me for a *woman* to be that casual about sex." If you point out to Bob that his attitude is just a tad old-fashioned and that it reveals, at best, some hostility toward women, he'll deny it. "I like women," he says. "But they don't think like us about sex. Or, at least, I want the woman I'm with to take sex seriously. If she's carrying around condoms, she gives the impression of being a party girl."

Self-Preservation

You'd think, though, that self-preservation would win out with men—that if they wouldn't use condoms to protect women from AIDS, they'd use them to protect themselves. But heterosexual men are just as capable of denying their own risk as women are. "I'm married now," says Paul, twenty-nine, "but I don't think I'd be worried about it if I were single. I'd *know* I hadn't slept with a man who might have been bisexual. But

119

women can't know that, so aren't they more at risk? I think they have more at stake in insisting on condoms." And some men feel that the issue of condoms—like most issues of birth control and sexual health—is the woman's responsibility. "I'd use a condom if a woman would just ask," says thirty-year-old Mark. "It's not a big deal to me." But would he ever bring up the subject? "I guess I just don't worry about AIDS very much," he says. "Wearing a condom is something I'd do only if a woman felt strongly about it."

That's just the kind of attitude that makes some women furious. "Sex and everything related to it is supposed to be a mutual decision, right?" asks thirty-one-year-old Dorothy. "But it never is. Men expect women to plan for these things and then when we do, we get criticized for it. We're loose, they claim, or too clinical or *something*. Why do I have to say or do anything? Why don't men care enough about women? The sexual revolution was great—for men. They could sleep with whomever they wanted, assume the woman was on the Pill and not worry at all. They've gotten this false sense of security that women will always take care of everything, that they *should* take care of everything. It makes me sick."

Changing Behavior

Early in the epidemic, many experts advocated a "talk to your partner" strategy, stressing the importance of communicating with your partner nearly as much as using condoms. "Research indicates that 'Know your partner' was very dangerous advice to focus on," says Rebecca Welch Cline, Ph.D., associate professor of communication studies at the University of Florida, and author of that school's AIDS awareness study. For one thing, you can't "know" if your partner has been infected with HIV just by looking at him or even asking about it. A study released in May 1991 by the National Center for Health Statistics (NCHS) found that 29 percent of the unmarried women participants did not think or weren't sure whether a symptomless, healthy-seeming man could even transmit the virus. (He can.) For another, "We've discovered that there is no relationship between people talking to their partners about AIDS and their using condoms," says Dr. Cline. "It seems that most of us, when faced with two pieces of health advice, will feel pretty good if we put into practice one of them at least part of the time. And, obviously, we'll choose the one that's easier. But talking is not a substitute for condom use; the two pieces of advice are not of the same weight." The NCHS study showed that the most frequent change single women are making in their sexual conduct is limiting their sexual partners to one man; while that's certainly a step in the right direction, simply shifting to fewer partners may not significantly alter one's risk of contracting HIV. "This 'Know your partner' business makes no sense since most people with HIV don't even know they have it themselves," says Karen Hein, M.D., who directs the Adolescent AIDS Program at the Albert Einstein College of Medicine/Montefiore Hospital in New York City. "To prevent HIV infection, women have to insist that their partners use condoms."

Intimate conversations with a partner may, in fact, do more harm than good, because they can be misleading. "What it comes down to," says Dr. Cline, "is that because women are socialized to be attracted to men who will talk to them, particularly about intimate topics, they will likely be attracted to men who will talk to them about AIDS. They'll think they may be safer than men who don't talk." But Dr. Cline's study revealed just the opposite: The men who said they talked to their partners about AIDS, but only sometimes or never used condoms, had had nearly 50 percent more partners than men who said they didn't talk about AIDS. Besides, says Tim Edgar, Ph.D., assistant professor of speech communication at the University of Maryland, "When people say they've talked to their partners about sexual history, very often they mean they've talked to them about a specific relationship. They're not asking questions or getting answers about AIDS-risk behavior; they're discussing the emotional ramifications of those earlier relationships." . . .

Condoms Are a Complication

Elizabeth, twenty-eight, has found that it's much easier to present condoms as a birth control device than as a means of preventing sexually transmitted diseases (STDs). "I have been pregnant twice and had two abortions," she says. "I even got pregnant when I had an IUD [intrauterine device]. So now I only trust condoms: At least I can see them and understand how they work. Men don't always want to talk about AIDS, but they usually will ask about birth control, and I just say, 'I want to use condoms.' Some men look surprised—my new boyfriend said, 'I haven't used a condom in twenty years'—but they usually respect my choice."

Both men and women agree that condoms limit spontaneity. "There are already enough complications in my life," says Lisa, thirty-three. "I don't want sex to be one of them. Using condoms is definitely a complication."

You could argue that AIDS, too, is something of a "complication." But Lisa, like many others, doesn't directly feel the threat of AIDS in her life. Like 81 percent of the women surveyed by the NCHS who believe they have "no chance at all" or "not much chance" of contracting AIDS, Lisa's knowledge about AIDS stays impersonal. "I don't want to die," she says, "but I know lots of women who've slept with more men than I have, and they're not getting AIDS. I think I have a greater chance of getting killed by a terrorist than dying from AIDS."

Even those who say they *are* worried, that they do see AIDS as a serious life-and-death question, occasionally "forget" their fears. "I'm in a serious relationship now," says Barbara, thirty. "At the beginning, we were very careful to always use condoms. But after a while, we both were having a pretty hard time insisting on using them every single time. A couple of months into a relationship, you both start to feel like 'Hey, we're in this for the long haul. We might even want to get married and have children someday.' Forgetting about condoms becomes an unspoken statement about the level of trust and commitment you have toward the relationship. You're telling the other person that you know that he or she will be there for you, come what may."

Institutional Changes Are Needed

Margaret Reinfeld, director of education at the American Foundation for AIDS Research in New York City, agrees that backsliding is practically inevitable because, she says, "People cannot live in a continual state of crisis. If you look at people who have been through floods and tornadoes, life begins to normalize in the trailers and shelters. People have as much of a crisis as they can handle; then they 'normalize' their life. This is not an intellectual decision, it's an emotional one."

Condoms Are Effective

Condoms are an effective means of preventing sexually transmitted infections with the human immunodeficiency virus (HIV) which causes AIDS. One single act of sexual intercourse or other high risk sexual behavior with an infected individual may lead to transmission of the human immunodeficiency virus (HIV). Condoms should be used by individuals at possible risk for HIV infection and other STDs, even if they are already using sterilization, oral contraceptives or any other means of birth control to prevent unplanned pregnancy.

SIECUS Report, November/December 1988.

So the trick, say the experts, is to achieve the state of mind in which safer sex is no longer a conscious decision at all but rather the norm of behavior. "You can't pass laws making it illegal to have sex without a condom," says Dr. Cline, "but you can work to change attitudes; in much the same way, public opinion has shifted through increased awareness of the dangers of cigarette smoking. Pro-condom advertising (like the banning of cigarette advertising on television) is a subtle, long-range tactic for changing societal attitudes; so are accessible, well-stocked condom machines. Changes in attitude often result from institutional changes."

Some of those changes have already begun on many college campuses. "My school gave out free condoms, which was great because then nobody had to be embarrassed by going out and buying them," says Kathie, twenty-one, a recent graduate of an Ivy League university. "Everyone I know uses condoms—for birth control, too."

A Serious Problem

Despite terrifying forecasts of growing numbers of people with AIDS, despite the well-publicized fact that women constitute one of the fastest-growing groups of persons with AIDS, many middle-class heterosexuals still do not accept AIDS as a life-and-death issue. As one woman who has worked as a volunteer at an AIDS clinic for gays puts it: "It doesn't come home to you until people you know are dying." But suddenly that's happening; Magic Johnson's admission that he's HIV positive may finally make us all realize that this disease knows no gender, racial or class boundaries. Maybe we'll finally recognize that all the talk and excuses are no longer enough.

"Imploring a heterosexual couple to reach for a condom before they have relations makes as much sense as telling them to wear crash helmets."

Condom Use Will Not Help Prevent AIDS

Don Feder and Ray Kerrison

The following viewpoint is in two parts. Part I is by Don Feder, a nationally syndicated columnist. Part II is by Ray Kerrison, a columnist for the *Washington Post*. The authors maintain that encouraging people to use condoms to prevent HIV infection is unnecessary and wrong. Encouraging condom use, they contend, perpetuates the myth that heterosexuals are at risk for AIDS and encourages promiscuous, premarital sex.

As you read, consider the following questions:

1. According to Feder and Kerrison, how does America's value system relate to the spread of AIDS?
2. What alternatives to condoms do the authors propose?
3. What specific reasons do the authors give for opposing condoms as a method of preventing the spread of HIV?

Don Feder, "Values the Answer to AIDS," *Human Events*, August 18, 1990. Reprinted with permission. Ray Kerrison, "Condoms No Cure for AIDS Epidemic," *Human Events*, November 23, 1991. This article is originally from the *New York Post*. Reprinted with permission.

I

Sometimes you have to pinch yourself to make sure you haven't fallen down a rabbit hole.

Massachusetts—Camelot of social trendiness, heartland of hemophilia—has contracted a terminal case of condom-itis. In the sacred name of AIDS prevention, the state will stretch latex advocacy to the limits.

"We need to normalize the use of condoms in society," declares Massachusetts Secretary of Human Services Philip W. Johnston. The state has unveiled a battle plan, which includes endorsing subway ads urging: "Put a condom between you and AIDS."

The commonwealth will pressure media outlets to accept advertising from condom manufacturers, develop radio spots targeting teens, ask theater owners to screen public service announcements, encourage bars, liquor stores, hotels and restaurants to distribute prophylactics to their customers ("ice water? toothpick? rubber?"), and beef up AIDS education in the schools.

It would take a Swift or a Johnson to do justice to the hypocrisy here—pure bushwah, and the politicians behind the campaign know it. It's a sop to the homosexual lobby, which clings to condoms as the simple solution to a disease transmitted primarily by their lifestyle. They will not be satisfied until every male in the land has a condom fitted at birth.

No Heterosexual AIDS

What divine derangement. There is no heterosexual AIDS plague; never was, never will be. Other than for male homosexuals, intravenous drug users, and their sexual partners, the AIDS threat is nearly nonexistent. Vis a vis the dread contagion, imploring a heterosexual couple to reach for a condom before they have relations makes as much sense as telling them to wear crash helmets.

Michael Fumento, author of *The Myth of Heterosexual AIDS*, notes that males can develop breast cancer—rare though it is. He then observes that it's statistically more likely for a man to contract breast cancer than to get AIDS from straight sex.

In 1988, the *Journal of the American Medical Association* calculated that the chances of a heterosexual contracting AIDS from a single encounter with someone not in a high-risk group to be one in five million. Yet the state of Massachusetts will waste a small fortune trying to persuade such people to don condoms as an AIDS preventive.

Nor are condoms a lifesaver for those who are exposed. Overall, condoms have a 10 per cent failure rate. For the young, it's almost twice as high. About 20 per cent of the batches inspected by the Food and Drug Administration a few years ago had to be recalled.

Condoms Do Not Work

When it comes to homosexual intercourse, condoms are even riskier—more prone to break or slip off during the act. "You just can't tell people it's all right to do whatever you want so long as you use a condom," says Dr. Harold Jaffe, chief of epidemiology of the Centers for Disease Control.

Dr. Malcolm Potts, one of the inventors of the lubricated condom, observes that advising an individual who engages in high-risk behavior to use a condom "is like telling someone who is driving drunk to use a seat belt."

© Bob Gorrell/*Richmond News Leader*. Reprinted with permission.

State sanction of condom use serves one end: condoning premarital sex. Kids who see government-sponsored TV spots promoting condoms get a clear message: It's okay to fornicate as long as you take the proper precautions—not the act, but its possible consequences, must be avoided.

Heterosexuals are more likely to contract AIDS from contaminated needles than from sexual intercourse. Can you imagine the Commonwealth of Massachusetts running ads which admonish: "Now boys and girls, be sure you use only clean hypodermic needles when shooting up!"

Condoms Promote Promiscuity

How many more have to die before our leaders get it through their exceedingly dense craniums that you don't fight a sexually transmitted disease by promoting promiscuity?

Today's youth have more information about sex, more access

to prophylactics, and a less-judgmental social climate than at any time in our history. Yet venereal disease, extramarital sex, illegitimacy and immorality are at all-time highs. What needs to be normalized in our society is the concept of premarital abstinence, the essential idea that sexuality cannot be divorced from values.

II

If first reactions to the melancholy revelation of Magic Johnson's HIV-virus infection are any guide, the United States is going to rush headlong into condom-mania under the national banner of Safe Sex.

We are about to adopt the utterly bizarre position that the deadliest disease of the age can be beaten with a 10-cent rubber sheath. Johnson himself promised to launch a national crusade for condoms. "I want everybody to practice safe sex and wear condoms," he said.

Health experts, activists, educators, the media and others joined the chorus, including New York City school Chancellor Joseph Fernandez, ever the opportunist, who invited Johnson to come to New York to warn kids they must rubber-up.

The message is fatally flawed. No one put it so bluntly as Larry Kramer, the militant homosexual activist, who said on "Nightline":

"Drugs are useless. Magic Johnson is not going to beat it. I would make this plea to him. He said he is going out to talk to kids about safe sex. It's a waste of time. There is no amount of education that is going to end this plague. The only thing that is going to end it is a cure."

Dr. James Curran of the Centers for Disease Control put it another way: "If you can control behavior you can control the spread of this disease and save lives."

Changing Behavior

Behavior has not figured prominently in the national discussion so far. But it's coming. Randall Pope, the AIDS-prevention chief in Michigan's Department of Health, says that if Johnson wants to help the young he will have to reveal his background with a candor not yet evident. "This is a time for complete honesty, complete frankness about how he acquired his infection," said Pope.

In his autobiography, Wilt Chamberlain, the former basketball marvel, brags of a promiscuous life of mind-boggling dimensions. He claims he has had sex with 20,000 women, the equivalent of a different partner every single day for more than 54 years. Chamberlain explained, "If the milk's free, why buy the cow?"

Chamberlain is a product of the Sexual Revolution, which began in the 60's and tore down nearly every protective moral restraint. The pitch was, "You can have it all, baby, without cost." Virtue, chastity, monogamy were labeled Victorian and junked. Today, the tab is in. It's staggering and still climbing.

According to the Centers for Disease Control, 45 million Americans are infected with incurable, sexually transmitted diseases—and that does not include AIDS. The CDC adds another 1.5 million for HIV and AIDS.

Sexual Excess

Larry Kramer thinks the HIV count is closer to six million. Sexual excess—homosexual to heterosexual—has taken a horrendous toll in the United States. We are now counting the dead in tens of thousands.

Yet false prophets are all over TV asserting it can be fixed with a condom. This is the greatest threat of all because children are being fed the lie that sex is safe with condoms.

In a report on contraception, the Alan Guttmacher Institute said that condoms have a 14 per cent failure rate in pregnancy. (Among homosexuals, the condom failure rate is 18 per cent.)

Condoms Are No Guarantee

Condoms are no guarantee against disease or pregnancy, and many refuse to use them no matter how many warnings they receive. Sex of this kind has its own emotional, relational and spiritual costs unrelated to the physical consequences.

Cal Thomas, *Human Events*, November 23, 1991.

Dr. Allan Rosenfield of the Columbia University School of Public Health told a Planned Parenthood conference that half of the three million unintended pregnancies in this country each year are due to contraceptive failure. So much for safe condoms.

Condom Failure

The *New England Journal of Medicine* revealed that in married couples in which one partner was HIV-infected and condoms were used, 10 per cent of the healthy became infected within two years.

Dr. Harold Jaffe, chief of epidemiology at the Centers for Disease Control in Atlanta, says, "You just can't tell people it's all right to do whatever you want so long as you wear a condom. It's just too dangerous a disease to say that."

Dr. Theresa Crenshaw, former president of the American Association of Sex Educators, Counselors and Therapists and a member of the Presidential AIDS Commission, told a House Subcommittee on Health, "Saying that the use of condoms is 'safe sex' is, in fact, playing Russian roulette. A lot of people will die in this dangerous game."

This is Magic Johnson's unprecedented opportunity. He can use his heart-breaking ordeal to persuade society to change behavior or become just another public advocate for condoms.

"Syringe exchange is easy, inexpensive and an increasingly popular AIDS-prevention strategy."

Needle-Exchange Programs Can Prevent AIDS

Claudia Morain

Claudia Morain is a free-lance writer in Davis, California. In the following viewpoint, Morain advocates implementing needle-exchange programs to help stop the spread of AIDS among intravenous drug users. Needle-exchange programs allow IV drug users to trade their used needles for clean ones. This prevents addicts from sharing dirty needles, a practice that has contributed to the spread of AIDS among drug addicts.

As you read, consider the following questions:

1. According to the author, how effective have needle-exchange programs been in preventing the spread of AIDS?
2. Why does the author argue that needle exchanges are necessary to prevent AIDS?
3. Why does Morain believe needle exchanges should be legalized?

Adapted from Claudia Morain, "Necessary but Illegal," which originally appeared in *American Medical News*, August 12, 1991. Reprinted with permission.

San Francisco—Pam, 42, is a heroin addict who belies stereotypes. Her shoulder-length chestnut hair is thick and well-trimmed, her striped jeans and casual brown sweater clean and attractive. She has a weary, intelligent gaze. You might take her for a burned-out community college instructor, or a tired social worker.

She has come, alone, to one of the most desolate blocks in one of this city's bleakest neighborhoods. Outside the iron-gated entrance to an abandoned brick armory, she falls in line behind a dozen other injection drug users.

This is the 14th Street outpost of Prevention Point, the nation's largest illegal needle exchange. For two hours two evenings a week, volunteers practice public health through civil disobedience: They distribute syringes, along with bleach, alcohol wipes, cotton and condoms, at two regular sites. A third team wheels a beat-up baby buggy heaped with needles along a route that starts at San Francisco's gold-domed city hall and ends a half-dozen blocks away at a seedy intersection in the Mission district.

Started in 1989, the privately funded non-profit program exchanges 9,000 syringes and serves about 800 IV drug users every week.

The Third Wave of AIDS

The first wave of the AIDS epidemic struck primarily gay and bisexual men. As the second wave sweeps through intravenous drug users—and a third wave threatens their sexual partners and babies—AIDS activists and health care professionals have set up similar illicit programs in New York; Berkeley, Calif.; Boston and Baltimore. Legal exchanges now operate in Seattle and Tacoma, Wash.; Portland, Ore.; Boulder, Colo.; New Haven, Conn.; and Honolulu.

And more can be expected.

The U.S. Conference of Mayors, made up of heads of the nation's 26 largest cities, voted unanimously in June 1991 to back legalization of clean needle distribution. "Now it's time for the federal government to follow the cities' lead," said San Francisco Mayor Art Agnos, chairman of the conference's AIDS task force.

Meanwhile, a New York judge issued a decision on June 25, 1991, that, while not precedent-setting, could encourage illegal exchanges. Manhattan Criminal Court Judge Laura E. Drager acquitted eight AIDS activists arrested for running an illegal street corner exchange. She ruled their decision to break the law was justified "according to ordinary standards of intelligence and morality," and constituted a "medical necessity," since 60% of the city's injection drug users are HIV

131

positive while only 40,000 treatment slots exist for about 200,000 addicts. . . .

The Efficacy of Needle Exchanges

Syringe exchange is easy, inexpensive and an increasingly popular AIDS-prevention strategy. But does it work? Over the past decade, researchers who have studied legal exchange programs in Canada, Great Britain, the Netherlands, Switzerland, New Zealand and Australia have generated dozens of studies.

"The data is quite consistent," says Don Des Jarlais, PhD, a member of the U.S. National Commission on AIDS. "Participation in a syringe exchange does not lead to any increase in drug use and does lead to a decrease in the sharing of drug equipment."

A case in point is Prevention Point. A study of the program by the University of California, San Francisco, presented at the Seventh International Conference on AIDS in Florence in June 1991, found that drug users who exchange syringes at least twice a month are three times less likely to share needles than those who don't.

Caring for Addicts

When you give addicts needles, you're giving them the right message—that someone cares enough to want them to stay free of AIDS, even if they continue to use drugs. Dead addicts don't recover.

Maia Szalavitz, *Village Voice*, March 27, 1990.

It would seem to follow that needle exchange therefore reduces HIV transmission, but that assumption is harder to verify through research. Says Dr. Des Jarlais, who is director of research at the Beth Israel Chemical Dependency Institute in New York: "Syringe exchanges probably are reducing the spread of HIV. But measuring that is a very difficult research proposition, to say the least."

Outside the armory, Prevention Point patrons aren't waiting for large, long-term, multicity studies before judging the program's efficacy.

Not Sharing Needles

"Never, I never share anymore," says Pam. That wasn't true when her choices were buying or borrowing. At $2 to $5 per needle on the black market, the weekly syringe tab for a twice-a-day habit can run as high as $70 if a clean syringe is used for each injection. "If I have $25 in my pocket, I'll cop [buy drugs]," Pam says.

Marilin, an obese woman with pale blue eyes and fine brown hair that brushes her knees, explains that drug-hunger drives even the fear of AIDS from her mind. "If you have a chance to get what you need, you're going to use whatever you have. You can't wait." Knowing this, she says, she hasn't missed an exchange in over a year. She and her musician husband now keep clean needles at home, and she tucks one into the ankle of his sock when he goes out.

Prevention Point is the creation of a loose-knit group of 13 AIDS activists, health and social service professionals and AIDS researchers. All got involved because they had close professional or personal relationships with intravenous drug users or people with AIDS.

The program has more than two dozen volunteers who work weekly, two-hour shifts. No physicians are among the volunteers; they have shied away from hands-on involvement with the program, though individual physicians have contributed money, and organized medicine in the state favors the concept of needle exchange. "We have no official position [on Prevention Point], but we support it as a stopgap until we are able to legalize their efforts in this city," says Steve Heilig, MPH, director of public health and policy for the San Francisco Medical Society.

Across San Francisco Bay, Kathleen A. Clanon, MD, is the sole physician-volunteer for NEED, the 10-month-old illegal needle-exchange program in Berkeley, which she helped found. After two years working in an AIDS clinic at an inner-city hospital in Oakland, Calif., the self-described "straight-arrow" said she felt compelled to act.

At the clinic she treats HIV-infected addicts, including some who don't learn about their infection until they enroll in drug treatment. "They're just starting to turn their lives around, and they find out they are already infected. That's a tragedy.

"There is an emergency," the 32-year-old internist says. "We have to be intervening with *all* the weapons we have in our arsenal. If we don't do something here, now, we're going to be like Newark in 10 years, and half the needle users in the county will be infected." . . .

Needles and Information

In San Francisco, police have largely left Prevention Point's volunteers alone. For their own safety, the volunteers always work in groups of at least three. One volunteer distributes clean needles and counts the used ones as clients deposit them in a fire-engine-red biohazard bin. Another distributes condoms and syringe-cleaning supplies. A third keeps track of the number of clients served and needles exchanged, information that is used by the Prevention Point research group at the University of California.

Volunteers are trained to provide drug treatment and health care referrals—as well as to give information about safe sex and safe drug use—if they are asked. But they don't distribute literature, or preach.

Anyone who shows up with a used needle is eligible to participate in Prevention Point. A strict one-for-one exchange rule is enforced, but there is no limit on how many needles may be exchanged. (Some people collect for friends and neighbors and arrive with hundreds of used needles.)

A volunteer team may see 300 clients in 120 minutes, with lines extending for almost a block. Each client contact costs $1.50. Each case of AIDS the program is able to prevent could save the system $180,000. . . .

Research Prohibited

In California, New York and nine other states, it is illegal to distribute syringes without a prescription. In 48 states, it is illegal to possess a syringe for purposes of illicit drug use. The U.S. government also prohibits funding of needle-exchange programs or research projects.

Many support those laws.

Lawrence Brown, MD, an endocrinologist at Harlem Hospital in New York and a senior vice president of the Addiction Research and Treatment Corp., testified for the prosecution in the Manhattan needle-exchange case. He argued that needle exchange only diverts energy from work that might accomplish real results in the wars on drugs and AIDS: providing education, health care and jobs to people in need.

Needle Exchanges

Recent research tends to confirm that needle exchange may reduce AIDS without increasing drug abuse.

With lives at stake and no other immediate options, the hard choice for needle exchange becomes easier to accept.

The New York Times, November 2, 1991.

The Rev. Amos C. Brown, pastor of San Francisco's Third Baptist Church, says he has attended four funerals of parents gunned down by their children for drug money. To him, the symbolism implicit in giving junkies the means to engage in behavior that produces such crimes is so offensive it outweighs any potential benefits of syringe exchange. "Passing out needles gives the wrong message," he says.

Treatment professionals also worry about the message issue.

David Smith, MD, founder and medical director of the Haight Ashbury Free Clinic in San Francisco, long opposed syringe exchange on grounds that it is an enabling behavior. "But in times of war, you've got to do things you wouldn't do in times of peace," the pioneering drug treatment doctor now says. "Syringe exchange, if coupled with education, can be an effective, low-threshold intervention to engage an out-of-treatment population." Dr. Smith stresses that he and his clinic have no official ties to Prevention Point.

The Medical Community's Response

The San Francisco Health Commission would like to see a legal needle-exchange demonstration project. Says Richard Sanchez, MD, the commission's president, "If we had the conservative wing of the medical community or the general public spend any time at all in an inner-city public hospital neonatal unit and understand the rampant problems—how many babies are being born drug-addicted and HIV positive—they'd realize something drastic and very innovative has to be done."

While the debate continues, traffic outside the armory is brisk. Young mothers bring toddlers; large families pull up in cars; sad, old men shuffle slowly into line. A homeless man arrives pushing his possessions in a shopping cart. A yuppie opens a handsome cigarette case holding six used syringes and politely inquires, "Who do I talk to about needle exchange?"

In barely audible Spanish, a shy woman in her early 20s asks for extra condoms. And a stocky young man, wearing spit-polished cowboy boots, a Giants jacket and reflective sunglasses, hollers "This is a bust."

"We are *not* amused," replies George Clark, Project Point's coordinator and only paid employee.

Low-Threshold Intervention

A master of repartee, the avuncular Clark exchanges friendly banter along with syringes, demonstrating that a low-threshold intervention is a subtle affair. In a few moments of contact, he hopes to make the ignored feel cared about and the stigmatized feel respected. He'd like to make the experience so positive that his clients will be encouraged to take responsibility for their health in other ways, such as enrolling in drug treatment.

But if they can't or won't, he'd like it if AIDS weren't the penalty.

135

"At best, needle exchange may help a handful of addicts."

Needle-Exchange Programs Will Not Prevent AIDS

Bonnie Shullenberger

In the following viewpoint, Bonnie Shullenberger argues that needle-exchange programs designed to prevent the spread of AIDS are immoral and ineffective. She maintains that while the exchanges may prevent a few cases of HIV infection, the programs send a dangerous message that drug abuse is acceptable and that society wants addicts to continue their self-destructive behavior. Shullenberger has a master's degree in theology and served as a chaplain in 1988-89 at St. Luke's Hospital in New York where she worked with AIDS patients. She is currently a homemaker and a free-lance writer.

As you read, consider the following questions:

1. Why does the author argue that needle-exchange programs are merely a media ploy and not a serious attempt to prevent AIDS?
2. According to Shullenberger, why are needle-exchange programs unsuccessful?
3. What does the author propose instead of needle exchanges to stop the spread of AIDS?

Bonnie Shullenberger, "Trading Needles," *First Things*, January 1992. Reprinted with permission.

It was the standard civil disobedience defense: they did it not for themselves, but in response to a condition of grave injustice and medical crisis. And the court agreed, finding them not guilty due to what is called "necessity justification" in New York State penal law. Who are these bold marauders, selflessly risking jail for others? Why, members of ACT-UP, of course.

On March 6, 1991, they boldly and selflessly set up a table full of syringes at the corner of Essex and Delancy on the Lower East Side of Manhattan. Boldly and selflessly, they had called the media to come and see them get arrested. Boldly and selflessly, they posed for the press outside the criminal courts building after their acquittal. Meanwhile, silently—and untouched by the police—ACT-UP has continued to give needles to addicts in Harlem, Brooklyn, the Bronx, and on the Lower East Side.

In her ruling, Judge Laura Drager admitted that "the defendants' actions would not end the [AIDS] epidemic." That was the understatement of the week, since they hadn't given away a single syringe the day they were arrested: the entire enterprise was nothing but a media stunt. Nevertheless, the judge opined, "the harm the defendants sought to avoid was greater than the harm in violating the statute. Hundreds of thousands of lives are at stake in the AIDS epidemic." Finally, she pronounced the law against possessing hypodermic needles "of limited, if any, success in preventing illegal drug use."

But is needle-exchanging any use in preventing the spread of AIDS? On the surface, it looks easy: give addicts clean syringes, and they won't pass a needle around, which means they won't spread the virus. This assumes, of course, that junkies are careful and conscientious people (like us) who will naturally be grateful for this kindly assist in health management. However, an addict usually isn't a yuppie. An addict has three states of life: stoned, searching, and sick. A person with a moderate habit might use a personal needle if he scores in a not-too-desperate searching state. A broke, severely addicted person who's in a sick state isn't capable of caution. Say such a person is a young woman: she might have to have sex with the dealer and a couple of his buddies in order to get what she needs. (This is a frequently cited scenario in crack circles.) That's when safe sex and clean-needle programs are about as meaningful as dust.

Needle Exchanges Help Few

Even though many people won't be helped by needle exchanges, some would argue the epidemic is so large and the risk so overwhelming that every possible point of attack ought to be used to try to save lives. There may be some merit in this argument, but it ignores the fact that drug addiction kills people, too. Keeping people addicted, albeit with clean needles, merely shifts the location of risk. Junkies get killed by dealers for not paying their debts; they get killed by other junkies for money or their stash; they overdose; they die of septicemia when their kidneys fail; they die of infections, seizures, and strokes; they die when they need emergency hospital care and the doctor can't find a vein for an IV or a blood transfusion. They are society's throwaway people, and they know it.

No one denies that there are not enough places in proven rehabilitation programs for all the people who are addicted. Motivated people who want to get clean have to linger for months until a slot opens. Once they're released, there is nowhere for them to go, in many cases, except to the same neighborhood and the same street corners where they spent years strung out. Furthermore, junkies are an unattractive, unstable lot. The likelihood that they would organize on their own for more and better treatment, and the likelihood that very many state officials would take them seriously if they did, is so small as to be unthinkable.

Needle Exchanges Are Ineffective

Allowing drug users to exchange dirty needles for new ones seems like an enlightened idea—simple, sensible and compassionate. AIDS is rampant among addicts who inject heroin or cocaine, and they transmit the HIV virus to one another by sharing needles and syringes.

But despite all the happy headlines and editorials, there is no evidence that this approach actually works and will reduce transmission of the virus. . . .

Clean needles, even if they could prevent sharing, wouldn't reduce a spread of the AIDS virus from addicts to people who don't use drugs. In the U.S. today, AIDS is being spread most rapidly by heterosexual contact, primarily through transmission of the virus from intravenous drug users to their sexual partners. Clean needles won't alter irresponsible sexual behavior.

Mitchell S. Rosenthal, *The New York Times*, August 17, 1991.

Yet addicts often have a certain clarity about their situation. Mary, a woman with a ten-year heroin habit who discovered she was HIV-positive two weeks before she was due to give birth for the third time, told me bluntly, "The day they legalize heroin, that's when we know they want us dead." Louie, a multiple-abuser who lived on the street in my Manhattan neighborhood, tried to hide his addiction from me. Finally I pointed out to him the six bags of sugar he put in his coffee. (Addicts tend to use enormous quantities of sugar in anything they can put it in; that's partly why so many have bad teeth.) He wept from shame.

Drug Addicts Cannot Be Saved

These aren't romantic tales. Louie was also manipulative and mean: one time when I took him to a diner to buy him a sandwich and coffee, he tried to rob me. I laughed later when I discovered it, because instead of my wallet, he'd lifted my purse-size New Testament. Mary eventually got into rehab but only after nearly killing herself in a postpartum drug binge; only after she was clean and in a daily HIV support group could she begin to make arrangements to give her children up for adoption. One man whom I visited through a long recovery from a cardiac membrane infection, during which he detoxed, wound up DOA [dead on arrival] three weeks later from gunshot wounds. Most won't be saved, no matter what we do.

Needle Exchanges Are a Placebo

At best, needle exchange may help a handful of addicts. It won't do anything for crack addicts, and it won't stop the suburban teenagers who visit shooting galleries as a nouveau form of slumming. Like our limited rehab resources, clean needles assist only a motivated minority. Meanwhile, what's the message to the larger community?

What needle exchanges primarily do is allow the non-addicted to shrug off the need for intelligent drug enforcement and readily available detox and rehab programs. The policy of the day is a "give addicts clean needles and give teenagers all the condoms they want" plan. Why? Not because these things work (efficacy is the "big lie" of AIDS policy). Rather, the policy is promoted because it permits the privileged to imagine that they're doing something really useful for "those poor people"—whereas what they are in fact doing is helping the afflicted to stay stuck in destructive and degrading behaviors. In short, we give junkies clean needles and we give inner-city kids condoms because we really don't care about them as people. When as a matter of policy we give someone that which degrades him, we admit that we don't think he's as human or as important as we are.

And when the courts let fame junkies like ACT-UP rewrite the law to promote their own agenda and have the nerve to call it compassion, we are eyeball-to-eyeball with anarchy.

Addiction Is the Real Problem

We as a nation have to care enough about the ruined humans who wander our streets in the throes of addiction to commit ourselves to fight the vultures who get rich off that misery. At the same time we have to provide plenty of opportunities for even the minimally motivated to find treatment. Finally, we have to begin to teach our children that enslavement takes many forms—drugs and sex are as cruel as the bondage slavery of centuries past. All I am saying, of course, is that it is necessary to restore serious ethical decision-making to our public discourse. Is that news? Will it bring out the press? No, but if ACT-UP had anything to do with it, I could probably get arrested for it.

"To effectively modify teenage behavior to stop HIV, a variety of approaches must be taken simultaneously."

Educating Teenagers About AIDS Can Help Stop Its Spread

Andy Humm and Frances Kunreuther

Andy Humm is the director of education and Frances Kunreuther is the executive director of the Hetrick-Martin Institute for Lesbian and Gay Youth, a social service agency in New York. In the following viewpoint, the authors maintain that reducing the spread of HIV among teenagers is an especially difficult task. While they support school-based AIDS education programs, they also maintain that other kinds of programs are equally necessary to modify teens' behavior, including making condoms available and teaching teens to counsel their peers.

As you read, consider the following questions:

1. What has been the general response to the subject of teenagers and AIDS in the United States, according to the authors?
2. What kinds of difficulties do Humm and Kunreuther cite in reducing the spread of HIV among adolescents?
3. According to the authors, how should adults augment ordinary AIDS-education programs to make them more effective?

Andy Humm and Frances Kunreuther, "The Invisible Epidemic: Teenagers and AIDS," *Social Policy*, Spring 1991, published by Social Policy Corporation, New York, New York 10036. Copyright 1991 by Social Policy Corporation. Reprinted with permission.

Much has been written about how the AIDS crisis has been neglected because it has mainly claimed the lives of poor people of color and gay men (of all colors), but little has been written about the constant spread of HIV among teenagers. In October 1989 the *New York Times* warned in a front-page headline that "AIDS Is Spreading in Teenagers, A New Trend Alarming to Experts," but the trend was actually far from new. Adolescents have constituted an estimated 20 percent of new infections with HIV since the beginning of the epidemic in 1981; what was new was giving the crisis among adolescents national attention. While those 13-19 years of age account for less than one percent of Americans with AIDS diagnoses, 20 percent of AIDS cases occur among those 20-29 years old. With an average incubation period of ten and a half *years* from time of infection with HIV to diagnosis with AIDS, this means that many young adults with AIDS—and some who are over 30—contracted their infections as teenagers.

Say No or You Deserve It

Only since 1990 have public school officials in New York City—the epicenter of AIDS in the United States—begun to treat the teenage HIV epidemic as a crisis. Schools' chancellor Joseph Fernandez's proposal to intensify AIDS education and make condoms available freely to all high school students provoked a rancorous debate that drew attention nationwide. The controversy is sure to be repeated as school districts around the nation grapple with this issue. Addressing HIV infection among teenagers means coming to terms with teenage sexuality, homosexuality, and drug use—topics that school systems and other youth-service providers have never adequately addressed. While many states mandated AIDS education in their schools as early as 1985, most of these programs consisted of "just saying no" to sex and drugs, focusing on transmission instead of protection.

Despite the evidence that HIV was spreading among teenagers, there was almost no push for more explicit and effective campaigns to contain it. Parents, who consistently refused to acknowledge that their children were having sex—especially with multiple partners or same-sex partners—or using drugs, did not fight for explicit AIDS education programs. To the contrary, they focused their protest on the presence of youth known to have HIV/AIDS such as the late Ryan White in Indiana and the Ray children in Florida, reinforcing misinformation about transmission.

White, a teenage hemophiliac, was hounded from his home in Kokomo and found much more acceptance in Cicero, Indiana. Yet even in Cicero, school officials made sure that he ate off paper plates and used a separate lavatory, totally misguided "pre-

142

cautions."

The Ray family had three young sons with HIV—three too many for their neighbors in Arcadia, who burned them out of their house.

© Steve Artley. Reprinted with permission.

School officials, fearful of controversy that could jeopardize their jobs, settled for moralistic programs that often did more harm than good in combatting the spread of HIV. The "say no or you deserve it" campaigns promote the misconception that AIDS is confined to certain "risk groups" rather than the result of risk behaviors *and* drives away youth who turn off to these constant messages of doom and self-denial. Students themselves were eager to believe *they* were not at risk, and in the absence of relevant and accurate information developed their own mythology of risk behaviors.

Adolescents at Risk

Teenagers have a hard time believing in HIV. Because of the long latency period, there are few adolescents with full-blown AIDS. Only a small number of the thousands of teenagers infected with HIV are aware of their sero-status, and those who know usually keep it to themselves or a trusted counselor to avoid rejection by peers. They are unlikely to appear on television or the news to talk about their lives.

Adolescents take risks as a normal part of their development, even risks with immediate consequence. We have found no magic bullet to keep teenagers from engaging in sexual behaviors resulting in sexually transmitted diseases and unwanted pregnancy; refraining from drunk or too-fast driving leading to accidents; or stopping drug abuse leading to overdoses. It is not hard to understand, then, why adolescents do not take seriously a threat of AIDS when none of their peers manifest symptoms of the syndrome. At a time when adolescents are increasingly uncertain about future opportunities, it is difficult to convince them to protect themselves from a virus that will not affect them for ten years. These youngsters find high-risk behaviors just another chance they are willing to take given their sense of the hopelessness of ever obtaining a safe and secure adult life.

Myths About AIDS

The image of AIDS as a disease of gay men and IV drug users has also allowed youth to feel invulnerable to HIV. Even teenage boys who engage in unprotected sex with other males may not see themselves at risk if they don't identify as gay. Others believe that they can't "get AIDS" from someone with whom they are in love or with whom they are in a monogamous relationship, even if they may have several monogamous relationships over a relatively short period of time. It is hard to counter these myths when the messages on television and from the government reinforce the idea that monogamy, marriage and love are equated with health while "promiscuity" and drug addiction cause AIDS.

Even young people who *do* have accurate information about AIDS find it awkward and daunting—as do many adults—to bring up subjects such as AIDS and safer sex with their drug-using or sex partners. Most have decided to take their chances rather than raise such uncomfortable and unromantic topics as past sexual experiences and personal potential for having acquired HIV.

And that potential is high. Nationwide, 57 percent of teenagers have engaged in intercourse by age 17, most with more than one partner. This figure is considerably higher in urban areas where there are the highest numbers of HIV infection. Sexually active adolescents have the highest rate of sexually transmitted diseases of any group, mainly due to the lack of sexual information and the lack of training on how to use preventive measures.

To date, the threat of HIV/AIDS has had virtually no impact

on the already alarming rate of teen pregnancy in the US. The same activity that causes pregnancy—unprotected vaginal intercourse—can put youngsters at high risk for HIV infection.

In addition, adolescents are the most frequent victims of violent crimes including sexual assault and sexual abuse (an increasingly common mode of HIV transmission). Survivors of sexual abuse are also harder to reach with HIV prevention messages, given the terribly mixed messages they have already received about sex.

The crack epidemic among teenagers is also directly related to the spread of HIV, since the use of this drug not only distorts judgment and leads to risk behavior (such as sex for crack itself), but creates an overpowering sexual need.

Gay Teenagers and AIDS

Finally, perhaps most ignored are the ten percent of teenagers who *are* gay or lesbian. These youth continue to be at high risk for engaging in risk behavior because of their isolation and low self-esteem. Fully 60 percent of young adult (20-24 years old) cases of AIDS are among males who have had unprotected sex with other males, yet this population is not addressed by the vast majority of HIV prevention programs, especially in schools.

For those who need actual HIV seroprevalence statistics to convince them, consider the study of runaway and homeless youth at New York City's Covenant House shelter where 6.7 percent of the clients tested positive for the virus.

Even the most comprehensive and society-wide HIV/AIDS education and risk-reduction campaign is not going to eliminate all risk behaviors. Parallel efforts must be stepped up to combat the poverty, racism, sexism, and homophobia that contribute to the behaviors. But as deep-seated and seemingly intractable as these problems may be, they are no excuse for not going forward with the best HIV/AIDS education efforts we can muster.

AIDS Education

Dr. Richard Keeling, of the American College Health Association, says there are two tests of a good AIDS education program: 1) *Did you involve the target audience in designing the program?* and 2) *Is it controversial?* If it is not controversial, Keeling notes, it is probably not any good.

New York City Schools' chancellor Joseph Fernandez knew very well he would create an enormous controversy by proposing to make condoms freely available to high school students. But the hard facts presented to him by his own AIDS Advisory Council made it difficult for him to sidestep this battle. While Fernandez could implement most aspects of his new AIDS education plan under existing mandates, condom availability required Board of Education approval, and that focused inordinate political and public attention on those little pieces of latex.

Even before the condom proposal was approved, Fernandez moved quickly to establish "AIDS Teams" (including teachers, counselors, parents, and students) in all junior and senior high schools. An explicit brochure on AIDS—including safer sex information and referrals for AIDS services—was distributed to every high school student within two months of announcing his initiative. Revisions in the AIDS curriculum for grades K–6 were completed, and revisions of the 7–12 curriculum began. Top staff from the chancellor's office were assigned to work with experts from his AIDS Advisory Council on moving these changes as expeditiously as possible.

Education Goals

Teenagers who are engaging in unprotected sexual activity now or who do so as they reach adulthood will be the AIDS cases of the 1990s. The goal of public health and education is to prevent those infections *now*. . . .

Any discussion of AIDS prevention requires open discussion of sexual activity, including sexual orientation, drug practices, and prostitution. Few teachers are comfortable discussing such issues. How can we expect comprehensive programs to develop without the aid of teachers who are willing to discuss the facts and the complicated social problems that are associated with AIDS? . . .

It is the duty of both state education and health officials to work together to develop AIDS education programs that will be acceptable to the community and that will halt HIV transmission.

Padraig O'Malley, *The AIDS Epidemic: Private Rights and the Public Interest*, 1989.

The chief recommendation of the council was to create a sense of emergency about AIDS among adolescents in order to help break through their enormous denial about their risk for HIV. Even the intense media coverage of the condom controversy assisted in the cause of alerting young people—and the adults with responsibility for them—that this was a crisis to be taken seriously.

As a Board of Education vote on condom availability neared, right-wing opposition to the plan worked to derail it by sensationalizing the issue. An HIV risk-reduction curriculum we at the Hetrick-Martin Institute use with high-risk gay and lesbian adolescents was obtained by an official from the Catholic Archdiocese of New York and leaked to the tabloid press, which had a field day focusing on such approaches as using zucchini or cucumbers to demonstrate proper condom use. This, the opposition said, is what your children will be exposed to if the chancellor has his way. The opposition also linked the chancellor's proposal with the gay groups that had been among those who helped develop it, singling them out as exploiting children and looking for ways to sneak into schools to encourage homosexual activities among youth.

In late February 1991, the Board of Education narrowly approved a new policy whereby condoms would be made freely available to high school students. For those of us concerned about the HIV epidemic among teenagers it was a great victory, but it was only the beginning of what needs to be done to stop the spread of HIV in this population.

Making an Impact

To effectively modify teenage behavior to stop HIV, a variety of approaches must be taken simultaneously. Most recently, community based programs have found that peer involvement is essential. The ultimate peer group, after all, is the two people who have decided to engage in sexual relations or share needles. If we can influence just one member of that pair to insist on safe (or no) sex or clean (or no) needles, we are having an impact.

Young people are ready to teach other adolescents about HIV prevention through peer education programs, teen theater companies, peer counseling groups, and AIDS activism. These peer efforts have the greatest hope for success. Young people are more likely to listen to other young people. Furthermore, the peer educator's participation in these projects helps cement his or her own commitment to the modified and safe behavior that he or she is advocating.

More emphasis in all AIDS education programs has to be placed on building the skills and fortitude necessary to keep encounters safe—mere information is not enough. And HIV prevention information should include lessons on the many ways in which sexuality can be expressed without risking HIV transmission, e.g., such "outercourse" activities as hugging, kissing, necking, petting, mutual masturbation, and so on.

Often overlooked in HIV prevention efforts among young people is the involvement of people with HIV. The chance to interact with a person with AIDS or HIV usually generates more questions from young people than any class led by an instructor who does not have the condition. It serves to humanize AIDS and relieve the isolation of young people who have friends and family members with HIV/AIDS.

Dealing with the HIV epidemic among young people is, obviously, not just a matter of instituting better prevention programs. There are thousands of adolescents living with HIV—most without knowing it. An increasing number are being made aware of their sero-status through testing programs that are voluntary or forced (for instance, there is mandatory testing when a young person applies to join the armed forces or Job Corps).

The increased number of youngsters testing HIV positive calls for adolescent-oriented programs. The issues of young people living with HIV are different from adults. Support groups focus on the needs of HIV-positive adults and do not address the concerns of a younger population. Some programs such as New York's Montefiore Hospital and those of us at the Hetrick-Martin Institute for Gay and Lesbian Youth are developing adolescent-specific programs for HIV-positive young people.

Accessing appropriate medical care for these adolescents is a discouraging challenge. Adolescent clinics originally set up to handle STDs [sexually transmitted diseases] and pregnancy issues are not always prepared to deal with the opportunistic infections that some of these young people manifest. Medical services that are good at serving adults with these infections are not trained in adapting them for young people. Finally, since many of these young people are disconnected from their parents who may have been the source of their medical insurance, accessing care can be extremely difficult.

Reaching Out to Young People

As the AIDS crisis continues into its second decade, we will see more adult populations either reaching their saturation level for HIV or making behavior changes necessary to avoid the virus. Adult gay men have already succeeded in lowering their risk tremendously. And in areas of the world where intravenous drug users have access to clean needles, they, too, have been able to keep HIV at bay.

But there is always a generation coming along that has not yet acknowledged its risk for HIV—a new generation of young gay men and lesbians, teens who are using intravenous drugs (including steroids and hormones) for the first time, and heterosexuals who are coming of age at a time when unprotected sex among heterosexuals is responsible for more and more HIV transmission. We need not continue to fail with this new generation if we recognize our mistakes and work assiduously to overcome the social obstacles that we have identified in reaching adolescents with HIV prevention education and treatment for those already infected. For it to work, all of us with responsibility for young people must play a role.

"*Abstinence and sexual intercourse with one mutually faithful uninfected partner are the only totally effective prevention strategies.*"

Abstinence Will Prevent AIDS

Ken Sidey

In the following viewpoint, Ken Sidey argues that abstaining from premarital sex is the only certain way of preventing the spread of HIV. Sidey is an associate editor at *Christianity Today*, a monthly Christian magazine.

As you read, consider the following questions:

1. What effect has Magic Johnson's announcement of his HIV infection had on American society, according to the author?
2. Why does Sidey reject safe sex as a way to prevent AIDS?
3. Why does Sidey believe sexual abstinence is the only way to prevent the spread of HIV?

Ken Sidey, "The Magic Word," *Christianity Today*, January 13, 1992. Used by permission, Christianity Today, 1992.

"Because of the HIV virus I have obtained, I will have to retire from the Lakers today." Those words, coming from the mouth of basketball superstar Earvin "Magic" Johnson, have probably done more to raise awareness of AIDS than years of lectures by public-health officials. In the days that followed Johnson's announcement, AIDS information lines were jammed with callers. Requests for AIDS tests doubled and tripled at some clinics. Even sports-talk radio programs featured doctors dispensing AIDS facts.

But as welcome as all that consciousness-raising has been, it has often fallen short of telling the whole life-and-death story of Magic Johnson, and of AIDS.

Johnson himself handled his shocking announcement with the same poise, courage, and spirit that pushed him to the peak of his sport. His desire to turn his personal tragedy into good for others is inspiring. But the message "safe sex is the way to go" does not say enough.

The 32-year-old athlete's initial statements skirted the issue of how he contracted the human immunodeficiency virus (HIV) that leads to AIDS. Before long, however, the rest of the story came out: In Johnson's own words, he never lacked for female companionship. In other words, he was sexually promiscuous.

Safer Sex

Some commentators have argued that *how* Johnson contracted HIV doesn't matter. Nothing could be further from the point. His life story is the only thing that can give substance to his message. How he became infected is important, not for the sake of condemning the man, but for the sake of educating others against the disease. AIDS is spread by behavior—most commonly through sexual contact with an infected person or sharing needles after intravenous drug use.

"Safe sex" is a misnomer. "*Safer* sex" is more accurate. Either version, in common parlance, has come to mean "use a condom." Yet again, that phrase doesn't tell the whole story.

The truth is, condoms don't work all the time. When used for contraception, they fail as much as 10 to 15 percent of the time. Some studies suggest they are even less effective in preventing infection with sexually transmitted diseases, including HIV, which can occur more easily than impregnation. Defects, breakage, and improper use all render condoms less than complete protection. "You just can't tell people it's all right to do whatever you want so long as you wear a condom," says Harold Jaffe, chief of epidemiology for the Centers for Disease Control (CDC). "It's just too dangerous a disease to say that."

What does work—all the time—is abstinence. One would expect that any preventive measure would be welcomed in the fight against an unfailingly fatal disease. Vice-president Dan Quayle tried to offer that line of advice following Johnson's revelation. "If there is something that I can personally do to encourage young people," Quayle said, "I would not say 'safe sex.' I would talk about abstinence."

Abstinence Is the Best Protection

There is now general agreement, even among homosexuals, that abstinence or exclusive contact with an uninfected partner are the only sure protections against the AIDS virus. Today abstinence and monogamy are no longer disdainfully dismissed as religious impositions. Rather they are seen as the pragmatic answer to a pressing problem, since the condom is admittedly inadequate. It may delay but does not prevent eventual infection.

At another level, there is even a growing appreciation that nature is trying to tell us something: that abstinence before marriage and monogamy thereafter are sexual norms which serve the survival needs of the human animal. Accordingly, the effective public health approach is not a nationwide push for a condomized society, starting with the very young, but a nationwide effort to curb the generation of multiple sex partners, whose primary source comes from the sexually active young.

Herbert Ratner, *The Wanderer*, June 8, 1989.

Quayle's message, however, was scoffed at by some, including Randy Shilts, author of *And the Band Played On*, a best-selling chronicle of the AIDS epidemic. Writing in the November 1991 issue of *Sports Illustrated* that featured Johnson's story, Shilts said, "Hardly any health expert believes that a message of 'just say no' to sex will do anything to stop the spread of AIDS. Young people are going to have sex. . . . Quayle's unrealistic proposal is not born of public health expertise but is part of the political agenda of the far right, which maintains that nobody should have sex at all except . . . on the matrimonial bed."

Preventing AIDS

Aside from Shilts's blurred moral vision, he is flat wrong about health experts. Former Surgeon General C. Everett Koop, who watched the ruthless rise of AIDS during the eighties, said that the best way by far to prevent AIDS is to abstain from sex until adulthood and to restrict sexual activity to a faithful, monogamous relationship. "If you are so foolish as to ignore that advice," he said, "the next best thing . . . is to use a condom." A bulletin from the CDC puts it just as succinctly: "Abstinence and sexual intercourse with one mutually faithful uninfected partner are the only totally effective prevention strategies."

Second, Shilts accuses Quayle of making a political football of AIDS prevention. But he is the one playing political games with abstinence. And he is not alone.

Less than two weeks before Johnson's announcement, the American Civil Liberties Union (ACLU) was taking its latest legal shots at abstinence as a solution for disease and teen pregnancy. The ACLU has waged a long-running battle against Title XX of the Adolescent Family Life Act of 1981, which funds high-school programs that encourage abstinence and adoption as an alternative to abortion. At first the ACLU tried to argue that the whole notion of abstinence was a religious value and therefore constitutionally ineligible for government money. Failing that, the group now charges that some programs open the door to religious values and is again seeking to drive them from the schools, in spite of the positive results they have produced across the country.

Rep. Pat Schroeder (D-Col.) led an unsuccessful attempt to cut the $7.8 million of Title XX funds from the Health and Human Services budget. By comparison, $162 million goes to contraceptive programs under other entitlement programs.

Abstinence Prevents AIDS

Critics of abstinence label it a "naive," "unrealistic", even "dangerous" approach to AIDS education. But the real danger lies in offering an incomplete solution (while excluding a promising one) to a killer disease. There are, in fact, several studies that suggest that among teenagers, easy availability of contraceptives actually increases sexual activity.

Fortunately, the abstinence message has apparently gotten through to Johnson. "The safest sex is no sex," he said two weeks after his announcement, "and that really is the most responsible choice." Unfortunately, his advice did not get as much media attention as his previous "safe sex" line.

Magic Johnson's story highlights the need for understanding of AIDS and compassion for its victims, whoever they are. But it also exposes sexual promiscuity for what it is: the major contributor to the spread of AIDS, as well as venereal disease and unwanted pregnancies. Promiscuity need not be accepted as a "given" in our society. Changing behaviors is a difficult task indeed, but it can be done—if we are willing to speak, and hear, the whole story.

Evaluating AIDS Prevention Concerns

Margulies 1987, *Houston Post.*

There are many provocative arguments debating how the nation can control the spread of AIDS. One method, illustrated in the cartoon above, is to give out condoms to young people so they can protect themselves against AIDS. Many people take issue with this practice and argue that it is encouraging promiscuity by saying to youth, "Go out and have a good time, and take these with you for protection!"

In this activity you have a chance to examine your values in the area of public health by considering methods to control AIDS and debating them with others in a group.

Part I

Working in small groups, and using the viewpoints in this chapter as a resource, indicate how effective the group believes each of the following methods will be in controlling AIDS. *Use a V for very effective, M for moderately effective, and N for not effective.* Consider only how effectively each method can prevent or control AIDS if carried out exactly as stated.

_____ require all schools to teach courses on AIDS prevention beginning in the fifth grade

_____ legalize homosexual marriages

_____ leave AIDS contact tracing and notification to individual discretion

_____ give out free condoms in schools and sell them in public restrooms

_____ provide clean needles in schools and in public restrooms

_____ tattoo all AIDS carriers with an identifying mark

_____ disseminate AIDS-prevention information through a high-profile advertising campaign

_____ use public service announcements to encourage all those at risk to get tested for HIV

_____ provide free, anonymous, and confidential AIDS tests in all public health centers

_____ require all major cities to institute needle-exchange programs

_____ let parents and the church teach children moral and sexual values

_____ make it a federal crime to engage in any activity that allows the AIDS virus to be transmitted

_____ practice sexual abstinence until marriage

_____ require AIDS tests for all marriage license applicants

_____ require an annual AIDS test for every man, woman, and child regardless of risk classification

_____ set up peer counseling centers in schools, community centers, public health clinics, and churches

_____ legalize drugs

_____ segregate gay and lesbian students in high schools and colleges

Part II

Using the same list, repeat Part I. This time consider only the moral or social values affected by each method. Indicate the group's consensus as to whether or not each method seems a morally acceptable way to control AIDS. *Mark A for acceptable and U for unacceptable.*

Part III

Consider both aspects of these issues and, as a group, decide which methods society should use to control AIDS. Each group should compare its evaluation with others in a class-wide discussion.

Periodical Bibliography

The following articles have been selected to supplement the diverse views presented in this chapter.

Jerry Adler et al. — "Safer Sex," *Newsweek*, December 9, 1991.

Sharon Beckman — "Court Finds Needle Possession Justified to Limit Spread of AIDS," *The Drug Policy Letter*, January/February 1990. Available from the Drug Policy Foundation, 4801 Massachusetts Ave. NW, Suite 400, Washington, DC 20016-2087.

Commonweal — "Condom Sense," September 13, 1991.

Edwin J. Delattre — "Condoms and Coercion," *Vital Speeches of the Day*, April 15, 1992.

Nancy Gibbs — "Teens: The Rising Risk of AIDS," *Time*, September 2, 1991.

Jeffery Scott Mio and Debra R. Applebaum — "In the Forefront of Our Minds: AIDS and Other Responses to Category Labels," *Journal of Sex Education and Therapy*, vol. 16, no. 2, 1990. Available from Guilford Press, 72 Spring St., New York, NY 10012.

Robert Noble — "The Myth of Safe Sex," *Reader's Digest*, August 1991.

Mitchell S. Rosenthal — "Giving Away Needles Won't Stop AIDS," *The New York Times*, August 17, 1991.

Jean Seligman — "Condoms in the Classroom," *Newsweek*, December 9, 1991.

Rod Sorge — "Drug Policy in the Age of AIDS," *Health/PAC Bulletin*, Fall 1990. Available from the Health Policy Advisory Center, 17 Murray St., New York, NY 10007.

Beverly Sottile-Malona — "Condoms and AIDS," *America*, November 2, 1991. Available from 106 West 56th St., New York, NY 10019.

U.S. News & World Report — "Teenage Sex, After Magic," December 16, 1991.

Jay Weiser — "Fight Back," *The Progressive*, August 1990.

Brenda Wilson — "Dirty Needles and the AIDS Dilemma," *Governing*, April 1992. Available from 2300 N St. NW, Suite 760, Washington, DC 20037.

How Can AIDS Be Treated?

Chapter Preface

Because AIDS is a condition that severely weakens the immune system and leaves the body open to a wide variety of opportunistic diseases, finding a single cure for it has been an elusive task. Instead, government agencies like the Centers for Disease Control (CDC) and the National Institutes of Health (NIH), along with private drug companies, have developed and adapted two categories of drugs to treat people with HIV infection and with AIDS. One category contains drugs that treat the opportunistic infections common to people with AIDS. The other category is made up of drugs designed to bolster the failing immune systems of people with AIDS thereby extending these patients' lives. The best known of the drugs in the second category is AZT or zidovudine. Other drugs include ddI, ddC, and acyclovir.

Most doctors have been pleased with the results of these drugs. According to Dr. Jay Lalezari, codirector of the HIV research unit at Mount Zion Medical Center in San Francisco, "Early results from a small study using AZT and ddC have yielded better results than anything else in the first decade of AIDS research." Results of drug trials from around the country, including a study done by Dr. Richard Moore of the Johns Hopkins School of Medicine in Baltimore, Maryland, show that AZT and other antiviral drugs have been effective at slowing the rate at which patients develop the symptoms of full-blown AIDS.

These drugs, however, have caused controversy for several reasons. Many people have charged that the drugs are harmful. Some argue that the sometimes debilitating side effects produced by these drugs—including nausea, diarrhea, and nerve and liver damage—negate their benefits. Others object to the drugs' limited effects—at some point the drugs stop being effective and the patient's vulnerability to infections increases. Still others contend that AZT is actually poisonous and destroys the immune system rather than bolstering it. Journalist John Lauritsen, for example, maintains that AZT is "the most toxic drug ever approved or even considered for long-term use."

Many AIDS patients who concur with Lauritsen have turned away from conventional, government-approved drug treatments. These patients are experimenting with alternative medicines and treatments such as Chinese herbs, acupuncture, nutritional therapy, and massage, among others. While many doctors scorn these alternative methods, others have begun to incorporate aspects of alternative therapies such as improved nutrition and acupuncture into their standard treatments. The viewpoints in the following chapter discuss a variety of mainstream and alternative treatments for AIDS.

"Therapy with zidovudine was . . . shown in clinical trials to prolong survival. "

AZT Is an Effective AIDS Treatment

Richard D. Moore et al.

Richard D. Moore is a Burroughs Wellcome scholar in pharmacoepidemiology and a physician and researcher at Johns Hopkins University School of Medicine in Baltimore. Moore and his colleagues tested the drug AZT on AIDS patients. In the following viewpoint, the authors describe the results of their study and conclude that the drug lengthens the lives of those afflicted with AIDS.

As you read, consider the following questions:

1. According to the authors, how did survival rates change for AIDS patients in the study?
2. The authors point out that other kinds of treatments used by the participants in their study may have affected the results. How?
3. What recommendations do the authors offer for the use of AZT?

Adapted from Richard D. Moore et al., "Zidovudine and the Natural History of the Acquired Immunodeficiency Syndrome." The complete article, with references and graphics, can be found in *The New England Journal of Medicine* 324 (May 16, 1991): 1412-16. Reprinted with permission.

Survival after a diagnosis of the acquired immunodeficiency syndrome (AIDS) is influenced by a number of factors. Early studies of persons given a diagnosis of AIDS before antiretroviral therapy became available suggested that age, the AIDS-defining diagnosis, and possibly sex and race influenced survival. These studies found little or no evidence of a secular trend toward improved survival. Therapy with zidovudine (formerly azidothymidine, or AZT) was subsequently shown in clinical trials to prolong survival. Studies of persons with AIDS, all of whom received zidovudine, indicate that survival is further influenced by characteristics such as functional status, hemoglobin concentration, and CD4 + lymphocyte count, as well as the length of time between the diagnosis of AIDS and the beginning of therapy with zidovudine. Studies suggest that the incidence of AIDS has declined and the survival of persons given a diagnosis of AIDS has improved since the middle of 1987. Several explanations for the decrease in the incidence of AIDS and the improvement in survival have been proposed, including changes in the surveillance definition of AIDS in 1987, reporting delays, and changes in therapy for human immunodeficiency virus (HIV) disease, particularly the introduction of zidovudine in the spring of 1987.

This study was undertaken to describe survival trends among patients in whom AIDS was diagnosed in Maryland and to determine how survival is modified by demographic and clinical characteristics, particularly therapy with zidovudine. This study uses data from the Maryland Human Immunodeficiency Virus Information System, an automated, person-based, longitudinal system linking epidemiologic information, vital statistics, data on inpatient and community-based services, and information from public and private insurance claims. . . .

Median survival increased significantly from 310 days for persons given diagnoses between 1983 and 1985 to 450 days for those given diagnoses between 1987 and 1989.

Survival and Diagnosis Differences

Additional analyses were conducted involving only the 714 persons in whom AIDS was diagnosed between April 1987 and June 1989. . . . Significant differences were found with regard to sex, with men surviving longer than women, race and ethnic group, with non-Hispanic whites surviving longer than minorities, and age, with those under 45 years old surviving longer than older persons. Homosexual men survived longer than those who acquired HIV infection through heterosexual contact, transfusion, or other less common modes. Those with an AIDS-defining diagnosis of *Pneumocystis carinii* pneumonia or Kaposi's sarcoma had a one-year but not a two-year survival advantage over those whose AIDS-defining diagnosis was another opportunistic condition. . . .

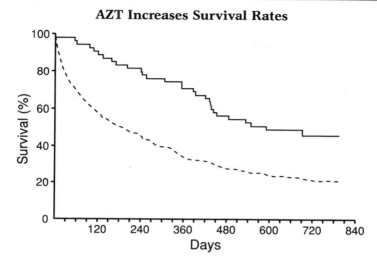

AZT Increases Survival Rates

——— represents the 56 people who first received AZT when AIDS was diagnosed.
- - - - represents the 362 people with AIDS who did not receive AZT.
These people were all diagnosed between April 1987 and June 1989.

This study was conducted to determine whether an improvement in survival over time among persons with AIDS could be demonstrated in Maryland, where a substantial and growing number of persons representing a broad mix of racial and ethnic groups, sexes, ages, and modes of transmission are infected with HIV. Using data from a comprehensive, longitudinal statewide information system, we found that survival improved most among patients given a diagnosis of AIDS in 1987 through 1989, as compared with those given a diagnosis in previous years. Homosexual men, non-Hispanic whites, young persons, and persons with an AIDS-defining diagnosis of Kaposi's sarcoma or *P. carinii* pneumonia survived longest among all those in whom AIDS was diagnosed in April 1987 or after. These subgroups were also the most likely to receive zidovudine therapy, the predominant factor affecting survival after multivariate adjustment.

Before the advent of antiretroviral therapy, studies found a relatively short median survival (11 to 13 months) among patients with AIDS, without trends of improvement over time. A more recent study found fewer reported new cases of AIDS than expected according to projections that used the back-calculation method to predict incidence among homosexual and bisexual men in three U.S. cities, although not among intravenous drug users. Statistical modeling suggested that AIDS therapy available since 1987 was the most likely explanation. In another study, survival among more than 4300 patients with AIDS in San Francisco was found to have improved in 1986 and 1987 as compared with previous years, primarily among patients in whom *P. carinii* pneumonia was diagnosed. For most of the study population the use of zidovudine was unknown, but in a small subset of 172 patients documented to have received the drug, median survival was 21 months, similar to the median survival of 25 months in the persons who received zidovudine in our study. National AIDS surveillance data also demonstrate a temporal improvement in survival among persons whose initial diagnosis is *P. carinii* pneumonia, though the effect of antiretroviral therapy cannot be assessed.

Use of AZT

By using a statewide data base that incorporates information from pharmacy claims and clinical trials, we were able to measure rather than estimate the use of antiretroviral therapy. Zidovudine is a relatively expensive drug that is unlikely to be purchased out of pocket. Given the high percentage of those with AIDS in this population who received coverage through Medicaid or Blue Cross and Blue Shield, and given our knowledge of the sources of zidovudine in Maryland, it is unlikely that more than a minimal amount of zidovudine use was not identified. The data indicate that the effect of zidovudine therapy may be even greater than previously estimated and suggest that we would have found an even larger difference in survival trends if more persons with AIDS had received zidovudine. In those not receiving zidovudine, median survival was less than one year—a figure comparable to estimates of survival in patients with AIDS before antiretroviral therapy. Because insurance status defined this cohort, the persons whose data we analyzed probably had similar access to medical care, as determined by the ability to pay. It is therefore notable that a large number of persons with AIDS (more than 50 percent) did not receive zidovudine therapy, despite its availability. These data do not address the reasons for the demographic disparities in zidovudine use. They do, however, indicate that race and ethnic group, sex, age, and possibly risk category can identify those who may benefit from targeting strategies to improve the receipt of medical care for HIV infection. In regard to race and ethnic group, our data indicate that minorities (predominantly blacks) have a shorter survival time than non-Hispanic whites but that medical care, including the use of zidovudine, contributes to improved survival similarly among blacks and whites.

AZT Is Successful

Retrovir [Retrovir is the brand name used by Burroughs Wellcome for AZT] is the first and only antiretroviral drug indicated for use in adults and children with HIV infection, and it has been commercially available in the United States since March of 1987. Retrovir is the most extensively studied medication for use against HIV infection in the world, both as a single agent at various stages of infection and in combination with other proven and experimental therapies.

Retrovir slows the progression of HIV infection, allowing asymptomatic infected individuals with impaired immunity (T4 cell count of 500mm or less) to stay free of symptoms longer and delaying progression to advanced disease for those with early symptoms. In more severely ill patients, it prolongs life and reduces the risk and severity of the opportunistic infections associated with HIV.

Burroughs Wellcome press release, May 15, 1991.

Several comments should be made in regard to interpreting our results. First, we did not assess the effect of the 1987 revised CDC surveillance definition of AIDS on overall survival in our study population. The revision could have biased the survival distributions in that more persons are now given a diagnosis of AIDS at an earlier stage of HIV disease, resulting in longer survival after diagnosis. However, as suggested in the study by G.F. Lemp et al., the effect of the change in definition probably altered median survival by only 20 days. Second, zidovudine therapy is likely to be a marker for access to other AIDS treatment, including other drug therapies as well as various types of home and community-based supportive care. For example, aerosolized pentamidine therapy, which may improve survival, was not included in our analysis because reliable information on its use was not available for the entire cohort. Third, our data are not designed to address certain clinical prognostic factors, such as degree of immunologic impairment. Several key prognostic factors were known, however, including AIDS-defining diagnosis, date of progression to AIDS, and principal risk category for HIV transmission. Another advantage is that the Human Immunodeficiency Virus Information System relies not only on reports of patients to the HIV Registry, but also on an intensive surveillance system. This serves to minimize bias from delays in reporting cases of AIDS. Many persons with AIDS "spend down" to a lower socioeconomic status, but the Human Immunodeficiency Virus Information System maintains longitudinal information on these people because of its access to data from the state or private and public insurers. Although relatively few persons with AIDS leave the state, care received outside Maryland is also recorded.

Increase Use of AZT

In summary, our analysis shows an improvement in survival over time among persons with AIDS in Maryland that coincides with the availability of antiretroviral therapy. Our data suggest that zidovudine (and perhaps other aspects of care associated with zidovudine therapy) has made a sizable difference in survival for persons with AIDS living in Maryland. The challenge now appears to be to increase the use of that therapy in all segments of the population infected with HIV.

"AZT is incompatible with life."

AZT Is Not an Effective AIDS Treatment

John Lauritsen

In the following viewpoint, John Lauritsen argues that the drug AZT should not be used as a treatment for AIDS. Lauritsen, a journalist, maintains that scientists have manipulated information about AZT to make it appear to be an effective treatment and have discounted information on its toxicity. Lauritsen believes AZT is a deadly chemical that harms AIDS patients. For this reason, he contends that treatment with AZT should stop.

As you read, consider the following questions:

1. How did the scientists studying AZT manipulate their research to make it appear effective as a treatment for AIDS, according to the author?
2. Why does Lauritsen argue that AZT is an ineffective treatment for AIDS?
3. Rather than using AZT, what course of treatment does Lauritsen recommend?

Excerpted from the first chapter of *Poison by Prescription: The AZT Story*, by John Lauritsen. Published in 1990 by Asklepios/Pagan Press, 26 St. Mark's Place, New York, NY 10003. Reprinted with permission.

Tens of thousands of people are now taking a deadly drug which was approved by the United States government on the basis of fraudulent research. That drug is AZT, also known as Retrovir and zidovudine. It is the only federally approved drug for the treatment of "AIDS" (a poorly defined construct now encompassing more than two dozen old diseases).

AZT is not cheap. Treatment for a single patient costs between $8,000 and $12,000 per year, most of which is paid for, directly or indirectly, by taxpayer money.

The Most Toxic Drug

The most toxic drug ever approved or even considered for long-term use, AZT is now being indiscriminately prescribed on a mass scale. Even the British manufacturer, Burroughs Wellcome, doesn't know for sure how many people are on AZT, but it may be as many as 50,000 worldwide. The great majority are gay men, but the drug is also being given to intravenous drug users, hemophiliacs and other people with "AIDS" (PWAs). Children, including newborn infants, are now receiving AZT, as are pregnant women who are "HIV-positive" (that is, who have antibodies to human immunodeficiency virus [HIV], which the world-renowned molecular biologist Peter H. Duesberg has described as a harmless and "profoundly conventional" retrovirus). AZT is being given to healthy HIV-positive individuals, under the pretense that doing so will prevent "progression to AIDS." Some members of the "AIDS establishment," like William Haseltine (of the Harvard School of Public Health), have gone so far as to advocate giving AZT to perfectly healthy, HIV-*negative* members of "high risk groups," such as gay men, to prevent them from becoming "infected."

The prognosis cannot be good for these people. AZT's toxicities are so great that about 50% of PWAs cannot tolerate it at all, and must be taken off the drug in order to save their lives. AZT is cytotoxic, meaning that it kills healthy cells in the body. AZT destroys bone marrow, causing life-threatening anemia. AZT causes severe headaches, nausea, and muscular pain; it causes muscles to waste away; it damages the kidneys, liver, and nerves. AZT blocks DNA synthesis, the very life process itself—when DNA synthesis is blocked, new cells fail to develop, and the body inevitably begins to deteriorate.

The cumulative, long-term effects of AZT are unknown, since no one has taken the drug for more than three years. Even if patients were to survive the short-term toxicities of AZT, they would still face the prospect of cancer caused by the drug. According to the FDA [Food and Drug Administration] analyst who reviewed the AZT toxicology data—and who recommended that AZT *not* be approved for marketing—AZT "induces a positive response in the cell transformation assay" and is therefore "presumed to be a potential carcinogen."

Peter Duesberg has called AZT "pure poison." AIDS researcher and physician Joseph Sonnabend has stated that "AZT is incompatible with life."

AZT Is Ineffective

The rationale of AZT therapy is simple, if not naive: the retrovirus HIV depends on DNA synthesis for multiplication, and AZT terminates DNA synthesis. Thus AZT should stop AIDS, if AIDS were caused by HIV, and if HIV were multiplying during AIDS. Yet there is still no proof for the hypothesis that HIV causes AIDS. Moreover, many studies show that no more than one in 1,000 lymphocytes are ever infected by HIV—even in people dying from AIDS. Since AZT cannot distinguish between an infected and an uninfected cell, 999 uninfected cells must be killed to kill just one HIV-infected cell. This means that AZT, as a treatment for AIDS, has a very high toxicity index. In view of this, there is no rational explanation of how AZT could be beneficial to AIDS patients, even if HIV were proven to cause AIDS.

Peter Duesberg, in *Poison by Prescription: The AZT Story,* 1990.

What benefits does AZT have, that could offset such terrible toxicities? None, as a matter of fact. AZT's benefits tend to vanish as soon as one scrutinizes them. The oft-repeated claim that AZT "extends life" is based on research that fully deserves to be called *fraudulent.*

The belief in AZT's benefits appears to be based on three bodies of "evidence." First are the Phase II ("Double-Blind, Placebo-Controlled") trials of AZT, conducted by the Food and Drug Administration (FDA). Second are anecdotal reports. Third is a report which appeared in the *Journal of the American Medical Association (JAMA).* Let's look at these one at a time.

(This section is based on documents that the FDA was forced to release under the Freedom of Information Act. A detailed analysis appears in my article, "AZT On Trial." Whitewashed reports on the Phase II trials can be found in two articles by Margaret Fischl and Douglas Richman in the *New England Journal of Medicine.*)

Phase I trials determined that it was possible to give AZT to human beings, although there was never any doubt that the drug was extremely toxic. The next step was the Phase II trials, conducted by the FDA at 12 medical centers throughout the United States, beginning in the spring of 1986. This "double-blind, placebo-controlled" study was designed so that two groups of "AIDS" patients would be "treated" for 24 weeks, one group receiving AZT and the other receiving a placebo. Neither the patients nor the doctors were supposed to know who was getting what.

In practice, the study became unblinded almost immediately. Some patients discovered a difference in taste between the AZT and the placebo capsules. Other patients took their capsules to chemists, who analyzed them. Doctors found out which patients were receiving AZT from very obvious differences in blood profiles. Thus, the very design of the study was violated. For this reason alone the Phase II trials were invalid.

There are good reasons why blind studies are required for the approval of a new drug. The potential biases are so great, for both patient and doctor, that a drug-identified trial would be scientifically useless. Patients who believed that death was imminent without the intervention of a new "wonder drug" must have been psychologically devastated to learn that they were only receiving a placebo. Physicians, with high expectations for AZT, may have been biased not only in the ways they interpreted and recorded data, but also in the way they treated their patients. It is noteworthy that the public has never been informed by the FDA investigators, by Burroughs Wellcome, or by Fischl and Richman that the study became unblinded. . . .

AZT Was No Miracle Drug

When the Phase II trials were over, most of the patients decided to begin or continue taking AZT. At this point the miracle was over. AZT didn't prevent them from dying. In 21 weeks 10% of the patients on AZT died (whereas allegedly less than 1% of the AZT patients had died during the miraculous 17-week treatment of the Phase II trials).

Another comparison: After the Phase II trials ended, AZT became available on a "compassionate plea" basis, and survival statistics were kept on 4,805 "AIDS" patients who took AZT. According to David Barry, Vice President in charge of research at Burroughs Wellcome, somewhere between 8% and 12% of the 4,805 "AIDS" patients treated with AZT died during four months (= 17 weeks) of treatment. In comparing the two groups—each consisting of "AIDS" patients treated with AZT for 17 weeks—we find an enormous difference: less than 1% died during the Phase II trials versus 8–12% (call it 10%) following release of the drug. (See table.) A difference of this magnitude cannot be due to chance—the most likely explanation is that the less reliable figure (1%, from the Phase II trials) is wrong.

There are still more reasons for being skeptical of the mortality data from the Phase II trials. The theory behind AZT is wrong: HIV (as argued persuasively by Duesberg and others) is not the cause of "AIDS." And even if it were, a drug like AZT, designed to prevent the virus from replicating by stopping viral DNA synthesis, would be useless, since in "AIDS" patients HIV is consistently latent and therefore no longer making DNA. On top of that, there is no evidence that AZT has any antiviral effect against HIV in the body, as opposed to the test tube. (For a while pro-AZT researchers were claiming results from the "P-24 antigen test," an unvalidated and highly inaccurate test, but such claims have been abandoned.)

Mortality Comparisons
(AIDS Patients Treated with AZT)

	Phase II Trials	Following Release of Drug
Bases: Total Patients Treated with AZT in Each Trial	(145)	(4,805)
Deaths in 17 weeks	1%	10%*

* The probability is less than one in a million that the difference (1% vs. 10%) could be due to chance. This powerfully implies that the less reliable figure (1%) is wrong.

Still further grounds for skepticism concern the ethics and competence of the researchers. People who would knowingly tolerate cheating, who would use false data, and who would cover up the unblinding of a "double-blind" study, would be capable of other kinds of malfeasance. There are many unanswered questions on how Burroughs Wellcome received exclusive rights to AZT, and how this terribly toxic drug gained government approval faster than any drug in the FDA's history. The National Gay Rights Advocates (NGRA) has charged "illegal and improper collusion" between Burroughs Wellcome and two federal agencies, the National Institutes of Health (NIH) and the FDA. Shortly after Burroughs Wellcome sent a check for $55,000 to Samuel Broder of the National Cancer Institute (part of the NIH), Burroughs Wellcome received exclusive rights to market AZT, even though AZT had been in existence for 20 years and Burroughs Wellcome had played no part in the drug's development.

Finally, the Phase II mortality data are suspect because the researchers performed no autopsies on the patients who died, and released almost no information on the causes of death. The FDA refuses even to divulge what cities the patients died in.

Summing up: It is highly unlikely that AZT extended the lives of patients in the Phase II trials. There are at least three explanations, not mutually exclusive, to account for the alleged mortality data. *One,* since the study became unblinded and the doctors knew which patients were receiving each treatment, the AZT patients, unconsciously or deliberately, may have received better patient management; the placebo patients may have been killed off through neglect. *Two,* the sicker patients may have been placed in the placebo group to begin with. (The FDA documents indicate that this was indeed the case.) *Three,* there may have been deliberate cheating: some dead AZT patients may have been posthumously reassigned to the placebo group. Given the sloppiness of the trials, and the deplorable standards of the researchers, the third explanation is entirely plausible.

Aside from the doubtful mortality data, there is the issue of AZT's toxicities. The FDA analyst who reviewed the pharmacology data, Harvey I. Chernov, recommended that AZT should *not* be approved. Chernov documented many serious side effects of AZT, and summarized its effect on the blood as follows: "Thus, although the dose varied, anemia was noted in all species (including man) in which the drug has been tested." . . .

A Philosophy for Recovery

To be honest, at this point we do not know exactly what "AIDS" is, or what causes it, or how to treat it (although physicians are getting better at treating the various opportunistic infections). From all of the evidence, it appears unlikely that "AIDS" is a single disease entity caused by a novel infectious agent, HIV or other. Rather, "AIDS" appears to be a condition or conditions which may arise from multiple causes. . . .

If "AIDS" is really a degenerative condition caused largely by toxins, both medical and "recreational," then what is an appropriate treatment? Not still another drug, but rather freedom from toxins. Long-term survivors, almost without exception, have avoided toxic chemotherapy (like AZT) and have opted for repairing their bodies through a more healthy lifestyle: exercise, good nutrition, rest and stress reduction, and avoidance of harmful substances (including cigarettes, alcohol, heroin, cocaine, MDA, quaaludes, barbiturates, Eve, Ecstasy, PCP, TCP, Special K, ethyl chloride, poppers, and all other "recreational drugs").

Human bodies are the product of millions of years of evolution, in a universe filled with microbes of all kinds; if allowed to, they know how to heal themselves. Recovery from "AIDS" will come from strengthening the body, not poisoning it.

"People affected by AIDS agree on this, that the single most important thing they can do is to keep a positive attitude. "

Positive Thinking May Help Treat AIDS

John G. Bartlett and Ann K. Finkbeiner

John G. Bartlett is a professor of medicine and director of the Infectious Diseases Division at Johns Hopkins Medical Institution in Baltimore. Ann K. Finkbeiner is a science writer and teaches at Johns Hopkins University's writing seminars. In the following viewpoint, the authors describe methods that people with AIDS use to deal with the emotional stress of the disease. Bartlett and Finkbeiner contend that a positive mental attitude can improve AIDS patients' quality of life and can bolster their immune systems.

As you read, consider the following questions:

1. What suggestions do the authors make to help AIDS patients improve their mental health?
2. According to Bartlett and Finkbeiner, how does positive thinking improve the quality of life for people who have AIDS?
3. How can good mental health strengthen the immune system, according to the authors?

Excerpted from John G. Bartlett and Ann K. Finkbeiner, *The Guide to Living with HIV Infection: Developed at the Johns Hopkins AIDS Clinic.* The Johns Hopkins University Press, Baltimore/London, 1991, pages 262-74. Reprinted with permission.

At some level, everyone knows that, as Robert Burton wrote in *The Anatomy of Melancholy*, "[In this life, we are] subject to infirmities, miseries, interrupt, tossed & tumbled up and down, carried about with every small blast, often molested & disquieted upon each slender occasion, uncertain, brittle, & so is all that we trust unto." One of the conditions of life is that we are susceptible and vulnerable, and so is everyone else we depend on. People affected by HIV infection know that their emotions—depression, anger, fear, guilt, dependency—though painful to feel and difficult to admit, are also realistic and perhaps inevitable. They know that despite the comfort of their friends and relatives, they must resolve these painful emotions alone. Their resolutions, though varied, are at bottom the same: somehow or another, they learn to deal with the conditions of life. The twentieth-century poet Randall Jarrell wrote a poem that answers Robert Burton:

> "If you are afraid of wolves,
> do not go into the forest," the Russian proverb says.
> We all live in the forest,
> and there is nothing to do
> but get used to the wolves.

What this means to people affected by HIV infection is that in spite of an inescapable infection and the inevitable accompanying emotions, they are in charge. They still make their own decisions and determine their own outlooks. "I'm made of good stuff," Dean said, "and the stuff I'm made of doesn't change because my situation changes." "Facing what I am up against gives me a new frame of mind," said Helen. "I expected a lot of life that I won't get. But I will do the best for myself and be an inspiration to others. I think we have more control over our lives than even we think we do."

No one says that finding a "new frame of mind" is easy. Helen said, "It's easier to say these things when you're feeling good." Easy or not, people do get used to the wolves, do gain a sense of control, do find a new frame of mind. They accomplish this with a few tricks.

Divide and Conquer

Cut overwhelming and insoluble problems into manageable, solvable ones. People have various ways of doing this.

Divide problems into those that have solutions and those that do not, and focus on the problems that have solutions. Helen had been thinking about dying and worrying about how her family would deal with her death. She could not annul the fact that her death would create problems for her family, so she decided to solve a smaller problem. "I am a real junk collector," she said. "I thought, if I died tomorrow, would my family want this twelve-year-old perfume? I've pitched out so much I didn't need. I had old *Family Circle* magazines since 1976. I went through them and laughed and laughed—at the prices, at the styles. I threw out two of my three corkscrews. I threw everything out. My surroundings are so much more comfortable, and now my family won't have to sort through all that junk."

Voices of Experience

Long-term AIDS survivors were asked in a recent study what they would say to someone who is found to have the infection. Their responses:

- Maintain a positive attitude (45%).
- Educate yourself about the illness (26%).
- Get good medical care (23%).
- Don't believe it's a death sentence (17%).
- Engage in healthful activities, such as rest and exercise (11%).
- Join a support group (11%).
- Get emotional support (11%).
- Be realistic/accept changes (9%).
- Get professional counseling (6%).

Robert H. Remien, HIV Center for Clinical and Behavioral Studies, New York State Psychiatric Institute and Columbia University.

Focus on short-term problems. Alan had been angry and depressed because he was just becoming established in his career when he began getting sick. After talking to his counselor and his partner, he decided not to focus on his long-term career goals—"I gave up on rich and famous," he says. Instead, he makes only short-term goals he knows he can accomplish. He has a kit for a grandfather clock he wants to build. He'd like to learn some Italian. When he accomplishes those goals, he says, he will make some more. He tries not to "get upset if the goals don't get accomplished.". . .

Give Your Feelings Their Due

When you feel bad, go ahead and feel that way. Tell yourself, as Dean does, "I'm just tired of this. I don't see how I can do it anymore." Cry, stare into space, refuse to talk, stay in bed, write your terrible feelings in a private journal—go off by yourself and do whatever expresses the bad feelings. "I don't believe in this crap of, 'You've got to be happy all the time,' " says Steven. "I'm not taped together as well as I thought I was, or more likely, the tape was old. Anyway, sometimes I fall apart and just feel awful."

In short, give your feelings their due. This is not giving in. It is acknowledging the reality and size of the problems you face. Somehow, such acknowledgement is easier than trying to control how you feel, or going from crisis to crisis and never feeling anything. These feelings, once acknowledged, don't last as long as you might think. They seem to wear themselves out and disappear. "After I've been feeling hopeless for a while," says Dean, "the feeling lightens up, and I feel that I've really got a long road ahead of me. I've seen too many people give up. I feel like I'd just like to keep going."...

Relabeling means redefining a troubling situation so that it seems more benign. Relabeling is related to thinking positively: any situation, no matter how bad, contains the possibility for something good. The idea is to focus on the possibilities for good and define the situation in those terms. "If I approach it with the right attitude," says Steven, "I can see the blessings."

Call something a challenge rather than a struggle, a preference rather than a need, an opportunity rather than a problem, caring rather than dependency. People who have to quit work say they are not losing their usefulness but gaining freedom and opportunity: the chance to volunteer, to read certain books, to learn to paint, to teach, learn a language, put together models, and especially, spend more time with the people they love....

Confront the Possibilities

Once, when Dean Lombard was in the hospital, he roomed for a while with a man who was in the advanced stages of AIDS. "I was glad to get out of that room," Dean said. "As long as I was there, I needed to confront the possibility that what happened to him would happen to me. But confronting that possibility seemed necessary, to deal with this disease as positively as I am."

Confronting the possibilities means, for Dean and others like him, understanding and admitting that the fact of HIV infection cannot be annulled. Steven said, "I have to deal with this whether I want to or not." It is now a part of life. So are the possibilities of fatigue, disability, dependency, illness, clinic appointments, and hospitalizations. And so are the emotional reactions to all this. "HIV makes me face things I didn't think I'd have to face," Helen said. Confronting the facts and possibilities and reaction is often the only way through them.

Confronting everything all at once, however, is overwhelming and unnecessary. Face what you are ready to face, and only when you are ready. When you are tired of thinking or feeling, stop and rest. Do not push yourself because you or someone else thinks you ought to be facing things. Face a little at a time....

People who focus on hope rather than despair may seem to be denying the facts. But whether denial is positive or negative depends on what you are denying. Denial is negative only if people deny the facts of their infection and live inappropriately: drink too much, take drugs, practice unsafe sex, avoid seeing a doctor, or preventing a person with AIDS from talking about sickness or death.

Denial that admits both the realities of today and the unpredictability of tomorrow is positive. Alan, who bought a new car on a five-year finance plan, is denying not infection, only knowledge of the future. No one knows what will happen or when. No one knows how any one person's body will handle HIV infection. No one knows how long he or she will live or what she or he might die of. "You really have to deny some of this stuff," Alan says. "I'm sad when I lose a friend, but I'm careful not to connect that death to mine. Death happened to my friend, and I'm sad about that. But it still hasn't happened to me."

Positive denial is nearly essential in dealing with this disease. If you don't know the future, you have a certain distance between yourself and the disease: you are much more than someone affected by HIV. Your life has many aspects, many parts to it, many things you are interested in, many things and people you love; and HIV, though important, is only one aspect of your life. "I'm not denying I'm sick," Dean said. "But I've made up my mind not to act sick, not to just sit around being a sick person."

Positive denial also helps people feel feisty about the disease. They feel like they are not just victims of some virus; they are people who have some say in how their lives are run. "I'm going to fight until I can't anymore," says Dean. . . .

A Positive Attitude

People affected by AIDS agree on this, that the single most important thing they can do is to keep a positive attitude.

During one of Dean's serious illnesses, he was near death. While he was recovering, he said, "I sat and thought, 'How long can I keep this game going, denying this disease? Do I want to continue? Do I have it in me?' Then I thought, 'I fought everything else, it's up to me again. I'll beat this too.' In a way, death would have been easier. But I think about what I'd have missed—the pictures of Neptune from Voyager, my sister's baby, my son growing up."

Now Dean says he concentrates not on what he has lost, but on what he has left. "I've become more conscious of the quality of life," he says. "Now I'm concerned with living before I die, and living *every* minute. Sometimes it's like a violent smack hits me: wake up and enjoy life."

Steven has feelings that are almost identical: "I don't know where my ability to enjoy life comes from. I love life so much, I want every minute. I keep myself occupied and my mind working. I compare myself to other people—I still have advantages others don't. I've been fortunate, and it's been a good life. It has been one big education. If this is all I'm going to get, okay. It's not bad. It's pretty good."

A Rich Life

I remember the advice of the fellow with AIDS whom I'd "buddied" a year before I got sick. "Get over your sorrow," he said, "it serves no useful purpose." By which he meant: don't deny your sadness, just don't wallow in it. He was right. In the hospital, when I explained to a friend how sorry I was that what we had shared in a decade of very close friendship would be coming to a halt, he would have none of it. "Nonsense," he said, "your life was rich and filled with music before you got AIDS and you'll find the way for it to be rich and full of music regardless of the nasty cards and handicaps you'll be dealt." *That* was a jolt. I decided to come down firmly on the side of life and of affirmation. I said "yes" to life. The possibility of death didn't have to terrorize my every waking moment.

Jody Maier, speech delivered before the participants in the Institute on Ministry to the Sick, Johns Hopkins Hospital, April 28, 1987.

Keeping a positive attitude can change the way people think of themselves. They think of themselves less as people with a disease and more as people who are—for the present, anyhow—alive. They say they know how to be alive and will live their lives the way they know how. They come to trust their own resources, to trust themselves. Sometimes they even become different people: "I've never liked telling anyone what's going on with me," said Alan, "but dealing with this disease has made me more open than any time in my life. I'm voicing my opinion more, am more self-confident." Along with that comes a better view of themselves: "I think I began loving myself," said Helen. "There's a difference between just taking care of yourself and loving yourself. I'm working on loving myself."

Keeping a positive attitude can also change the way people feel about the future. "I think a person should feel everything in life," Alan said, "even the negative things. But I tell myself I'm fine and I'm going to be fine as long as I can. I have this feeling, I could be here when a cure comes. I'm very strong." Helen says she's never going to settle for less than she can have. Dean says he doesn't know what will happen in the months ahead, but he doesn't want to give up: "I've worked too hard, I'm a good person, and I have a will power that won't quit. I want to make something positive out of something negative."

Dean has a motto he uses to keep himself active and interested in life: "A body at rest stays at rest," he says, "and a body in motion stays in motion." He borrowed the motto from his high-school physics class and, he says, "I say it over and over. I use it to think myself well."

People come to believe that life need not be perfect or infinite to be good, and that hope can come in little packets and delight can come from little things. "I've been able to cope and feel happy and delighted about living," said June. "A lot has to do with your attitude toward life. You like it or you don't."

The Mind-Body Connection

Your attitude toward life might in fact be related to your health. A field of research studies the intricate connections between mental state, the brain, and the immune system. The field goes by two impossible names: one is *neuroimmunomodulation*, the other is *psychoneuroimmunology*.

Specifically, stress seems to affect the immune system's ability to respond to infection. Several studies selected people under certain kinds of stresses: people whose spouses had died, people with severe depression, medical students at examination time, people under such extreme physical stresses as marathon running or dieting to the point of malnutrition. Their blood was analyzed for changes in immune response, that is, for changes in certain cells of the immune system: T cells, B cells, and white blood cells called natural killer cells.

Different studies measured immune response differently. In some studies, researchers counted the numbers of T and B cells in the blood. In others, researchers treated people's T cells with a chemical that stimulates reproduction, then counted the numbers of new T cells. In still others, researchers added natural killer cells to foreign cells, then measured the number of foreign cells not killed.

Regardless of which measure of immune response was studied, most researchers found that people under stress have immune responses that are somewhat lower than the immune systems of people not under stress. In other words, people under stress have fewer of certain immune system cells, or they have cells that reproduce less successfully, or they have cells that respond ineffectively to foreign cells.

The converse is also true: not only do people under stress have lower immune responses, but people with positive attitudes seem to have better immune responses. Some studies, done specifically on people with HIV infection, found that those who describe themselves as vigorous and self-expressive, who have ways of venting their emotions, and who exercise regularly have better immune responses. The level of T cell reproduction and the response of the natural killer cells—the same measures of immune response that had been lower with stressed people—were higher.

Other researchers have suggested theories of how stress might affect immune response. In other words, all these theories suggest how a person's mental state and the immune system might be linked. When people are under stress, their adrenal glands release hormones called *glucocorticoids* (the medications cortisone and prednisone are examples of glucocorticoids). In the immune system, glucocorticoids inhibit the release of chemicals called *interferon* and *interleukin-2*, which immune cells use to fight off fungi, bacteria, and viruses. In the bloodstream, glucocorticoids also decrease, temporarily at least, the number of certain T cells called T4 or CD4 cells, the same cells that HIV preferentially infects. And in experiments in the laboratory, another hormone the adrenal gland releases under stress, called *adrenaline* or *epinephrine*, seems to suppress reproduction of CD4 cells. In any case, because HIV specifically infects CD4 cells, anything that suppresses CD4 cells might make matters worse for someone trying to combat HIV infections.

It is hard to draw conclusions from any of these studies. The experiments with CD4 cells were done on animals or in laboratory dishes and not on living humans. The studies on humans measured different aspects of the immune system's response, they did not exclude people who were not eating and sleeping, they measured stress differently, and the stresses themselves were different and of different magnitudes.

Most importantly, many of the changes measured were small, and no one knows whether small changes in immune response are clinically important—that is, whether they actually increase the chances of getting sick. In general, take the research with a grain of salt: this field is only a few years old; it connects psychology, the brain, and the immune system; and all three systems are extraordinarily complex and not yet understood.

In spite of the studies' inconclusiveness, however, the sense in this new field is that people who are more emotionally stable may be less vulnerable to disease. When sick, they seem to do better, become less severely sick, stay alive longer.

"Nutritional approaches might represent an essential public-health defense against an epidemic that pushes to the limit our will to prevail. "

Changing Dietary Habits May Help Treat AIDS

Kirk Johnson

Kirk Johnson is a contributing editor for *East West*, a monthly natural health magazine. In the following viewpoint, Johnson contends that diet and nutrition might be factors in treating AIDS. By choosing a healthy and nutritious diet, people with AIDS may strengthen their immune systems' ability to fight off opportunistic infections and prevent other infections from starting, Johnson argues.

As you read, consider the following questions:

1. What factors led some researchers to study the relationship between AIDS and nutrition, according to Johnson?
2. According to the author, what kinds of diets and supplements do researchers recommend to treat AIDS?
3. What kind of opposition to using nutrition as a treatment for AIDS does the author discuss?

Fearing he is losing the battle against AIDS, a desperate young man sits on a plane bound for Israel—and, he hopes, a new life. For several months he has fought fevers, pneumonia, and weight loss in a losing duel with a virus researchers say is unstoppable. His hope rests on a product called AL-721, a lecithin derivative made from egg yolks, that is not yet sold in the United States.

After two weeks of treatment, his diarrhea abates and his appetite returns. Another two weeks go by and he begins to gain weight. After two and a half months, he returns home, mimicking AL-721 treatments with a daily regimen of granulated lecithin and egg yolk. His sores and rashes disappear, and his T-4 count, a prime measure of immune-system health, rises.

Nutritional Approaches

AL-721 is but one of a number of nutritional approaches that are slowly forcing a reconsideration of the notion that, in the absence of a vaccine that will cure AIDS outright, humankind is impotent to halt the progression of the disease. AIDS still is frighteningly deadly; many who develop it suffer terribly and die within two years of diagnosis. But some persons with AIDS are living active, vibrant lives five or more years after diagnosis.

Of these, many stand by alternative remedies, a constellation of approaches full of promise. Witness Compound Q, an extract of the Chinese herb *Trichosanthes kirilowii*, which has been shown in laboratory experiments to selectively destroy immune-system cells infected with the human immunodeficiency virus (HIV), thus achieving a goal unmatched by most advanced experimental drugs.

Alternative approaches to AIDS are also being explored by practitioners of a burgeoning medical specialty called psychoneuroimmunology, which studies connections between the mind and the body. At the 1988 annual meeting of the American Association for the Advancement of Science, researchers from three separate medical centers presented experimental findings that stress reduction and social support had a measurable, positive impact on the immune-system vitality of dozens of men with AIDS.

It is in the science of nutrition that we find one of hope's most stirring calls. Because the immune mechanism, like every bodily system, feeds on nutrients, increasing numbers of investigators are inquiring into the possibility that good nutrition may slow the normally rapid deterioration in health seen in people with AIDS. There is even speculation that adequate nutrition may actually prevent HIV-infected persons from developing AIDS. If so, nutritional approaches might represent an essential public-health defense against an epidemic that pushes to the limit our will to prevail—and tests our belief in hope.

Intravenous drug abusers, gay men, and Haitians may appear wholly disparate: they are affluent and poor, black and brown and white, and urban and rural dwellers. Yet James Hebert suspects that all major categories of people susceptible to AIDS infection are bound by a common connection: compromised nutrition.

Hebert, a nutritional epidemiologist with the University of Massachusetts Medical School in Worcester, begins his argument by departing sharply from the popular focus on minimizing exposure to the AIDS virus. "Safe sex" campaigns, needle exchange programs, and monogamy may have a place in halting the spread of this epidemic, he reasons, but exposure to a pathogen is only one of the factors that determines risk of contracting an infectious disease. The other is the resistance of the organism coming in contact with the infectious agent. And on that score, nutrition may play a major role.

Consider the nutritional handicaps that beset intravenous drug abusers, whose highly processed diets often lack protein and vitamins. Most IV drug users have poor appetites and erratic eating habits, and tend to absorb nutrients poorly, in part because of digestive disorders.

These problems have a direct impact on immune function. Lack of dietary protein is responsible for a condition known as protein energy malnutrition (PEM), which has a devastating effect on the structure and function of the thymus gland. The thymus, a small spongy organ that resides beneath the breastbone, is charged with churning out T-cells, also called T lymphocytes. The thymus is a linchpin for immunity; its T-cells play a major part in fighting bacterial and viral infections. People who are malnourished have below-normal numbers of circulating T-cells and might subsequently be unable to fend off the HIV that is responsible for AIDS.

Effects of Poverty-Level Diets

In addition, IV drug abusers are usually poor, and the nutritional and immunological problems that beset people living in poverty are well established. The sub-par nutrient levels that mark poverty-level diets contribute to vitamin and mineral deficiencies in addition to PEM. These deficiencies, in turn, can cause immune dysfunction. . . .

If malnutrition might help to explain the preponderance of AIDS in Caribbean and African nations, and among drug abusers and other low-income Americans, then what about gay men? Many gays are affluent enough to slip past the nutritional shortcomings of a poverty-level diet. One reader survey for the gay newspaper *The Advocate* carries the headline: "Exceptional spending ability at a relatively young age." Hebert reasons that for these affluent urbanites, frequent exposure to the AIDS virus may be a weightier risk factor than the integrity of the body's defenses against it. Still, some immune-system problems results from too *many* nutrients. This is especially true of fats. Excess polyunsaturated fats may indirectly suppress the level of natural killer cells, large granular complexes that attack certain viruses. Likewise, cholesterol, once it is oxidized in the body, is highly immunosuppressive. Hence, a diet rich in meats, refined carbohydrates, and fats and oils—the standard fare of affluent America—could predispose one to immune problems. . . .

AIDS and Nutrition: A Summary of Selected Findings

Researcher	Year	Principal Finding
Jain & Chandra	1984	Similar immune changes are seen in persons with AIDS and those with immune deficiencies.
Hebert	1988	Inadequate diet could be a factor linking all groups susceptible to AIDS.
Hickson	1989	Proper nutrition may prevent immune breakdown that transforms HIV infection to AIDS.
Winick	1989	AIDS patients should eat as much as possible to guard against malnourishment.
Bogden	1990	HIV-positive patients have below-normal levels of six nutrients considered important to immune function.
Standish	1990	Holistic approaches, including whole foods and nutrition supplements, appear valuable for HIV patients with ARC (preliminary findings).
Levy	ongoing since mid-1980s	Macrobiotic regimen boosts immune function and emotional health of persons with AIDS.

Kirk Johnson, *East West*, February 1991.

Hebert is by no means the only researcher to sound the nutrition alarm. From Memorial University of Newfoundland, V. K. Jain, and R. K. Chandra, M.D., report startling parallels between the immunologic abnormalities in AIDS patients and the immune changes seen during nutrient deficiencies. Writing in

Nutrition Research, they compare the increase, decrease, or presence of seventeen crucial immune-system components observed in persons with AIDS and the status of those markers in persons with protein energy malnutrition. The coincidence is remarkable: for fourteen of the seventeen criteria, the immune-system changes seen in AIDS and PEM are similar. And of the three that remain, there is insufficient information to make an adequate comparison for two. . . .

Nutritional Status Linked to Survival

UCLA School of Medicine researcher Rowan Chlebowski, M.D., Ph.D., and colleagues reported a study designed to assess the relationships between nutritional status, common AIDS-related gastrointestinal problems (such as nausea, weight loss, and diarrhea), and length of survival among seventy-one AIDS patients. Most subjects were receiving a standard American diet, sometimes bolstered by supplements.

One of Chlebowski's findings was a striking relationship between nutritional status, as measured by the level of serum albumin, and survival. (Albumin, a blood protein manufactured in the liver, is a conventional marker of nutritional vitality.) Patients who began the study with normal albumin levels (more than 3.5 grams per deciliter) survived an average of 960 days. In contrast, those who started with greatly reduced albumin levels (roughly 2.5 grams per deciliter or less) survived only seventeen days. "We found that AIDS infection has a drastic impact on nutritional status," Chlebowski told *East West*. "What's still not clear is whether boosting a person's nutritional status helps them fight the AIDS infection." Nonetheless, Chlebowski says, the suggestion based on his study that some sort of supplementation to maintain normal albumin levels might be beneficial against AIDS is "a reasonable hypothesis.". . .

For a variety of reasons, growing numbers of nutritionists, physicians, patient advocates, and others are beginning to press for aggressive nutritional support for persons with AIDS. Some researchers, although an apparent minority, believe in the probability that intervention with the right nutrients might prevent or delay a breakdown in immune defenses. . . .

Doctors' Stories

Their remedies may be unconventional, but to hear these doctors tell the story, so may be their results. Robert F. Cathcart III, M.D., of San Mateo, California, may typify much of the promise—and the frustration—that embodies this school of approaches to AIDS. Cathcart, a Stanford-trained allergist and orthomolecular physician, believes that while massive doses of vitamin C cannot cure AIDS, it can maintain high levels of health in AIDS patients for an extended period of time, thereby enabling patients to avoid multiple and costly hospitalization and "at least doubling their life expectancy" after diagnosis. And he claims to have the patient histories to prove it.

Cathcart's Achilles heel is the strength of his evidence. Clinical nutritionist Joan Taber noted in *AIDS Patient Care* that Cathcart's careful work is a collection of individual case histories rather than a formal study, which would typically involve placebos, a control group, and double-blind evaluation. As a result, it is impossible to determine whether the beneficial changes seen in his patients might be caused by the power of suggestion, Cathcart's own reporting bias, the other vitamins and minerals he prescribes, or unrelated factors, such as the patients' concomitant use of the experimental drug AZT, creative visualization, or other therapeutic approaches.

Enhancing Immune Function

The sciences of nutrition and psychoneuroimmunology suggest that a healthy diet and positive attitude can do much to enhance immune function, even for those who face a life-threatening illness such as AIDS.

Tom Monte, *The Way of Hope*, 1989.

It is a weakness Cathcart freely admits. "I haven't had the staff or the money to investigate this phenomenon rigorously," Cathcart says. "It's been difficult enough to maintain a medical practice. When people find out you're prescribing vitamin C, they assume you're a quack and you start losing patient referrals."

Cathcart's dilemma is no doubt shared by many other practitioners who believe in alternative approaches yet are met by mainstream indifference (or hostility) but few offers to subject the approaches to rigorous trials. Because such tests represent investments of time and dollars that usually lie beyond the reach of individuals, institutional lack of interest means that government or foundation support is unlikely. Thus critics can continue to insist that alternative therapies are untested, a charge usually, though probably unfairly, interpreted as synonymous with "invalid."

Against this tide, however, stand two research projects currently investigating the role of whole foods and vitamin/mineral supplementation as a tool in the treatment of AIDS. "Most of the mainstream research that's been done on nutritional approaches zeroes in on single nutrients," says Leanna Standish, Ph.D., director of research at John Bastyr College of

Naturopathic Medicine, in Seattle. "These two projects are among the few ongoing works to investigate the value of a more holistic regimen."

Standish and colleagues at Bastyr are conducting one of the studies, a one-year clinical trial involving thirty-two HIV-infected patients with AIDS-related complex or ARC, a condition involving some but not all of the symptoms of AIDS. It is a multi-pronged inquiry encompassing not just nutrition, but botanical medicine, homeopathy, hydrotherapy, and psychotherapy. The approach may obscure the precise effects, if any, of a single therapy, but Standish says such a pristine assessment lies beyond the scope of her work. "We're trying to answer the question, 'Does a holistic state-of-the-art therapeutic approach benefit these patients?' "

Natural vs. Conventional Therapies

The nutritional component of the Bastyr study uses education (patient diaries and nutritional counseling), computer analysis (to determine each patient's nutrient intake), and high-quality multivitamins. Patients take large doses of nutrients in which they are deficient and are given substantial amounts of beta carotene and vitamin C. Patients are also encouraged to decrease their consumption of sugar and caffeine, to increase their intake of complex carbohydrates, and to eat more whole foods, "though we're not rigid about vegetarianism," says Standish.

The project is designed to closely parallel a research project at Seattle's Harborview Hospital, where ARC patients are involved in a study of AZT. Standish hopes the outcome will give the medical community its first solid glimpse of how the best natural therapies compare with the best conventional approach. By comparing one therapy with another Standish obviates the need for a control group, thus sidestepping the thorny ethics of administering a placebo to persons with a terminal disease. . . . Preliminary results "have been very exciting. None of the patients moved into AIDS, and that's significant. Across the board, there's been significant clinical improvement," says Standish. "Patients look better and say they feel better." . . .

A Macrobiotic Regimen

The second ongoing test of the value of alternative nutritional therapies is a six-year-old investigation of a macrobiotic regimen being conducted at the Boston University Medical School. Although the study has weaknesses, it provided an encouraging glimpse of the possible value of the macrobiotic approach.

Macrobiotics is a philosophy that stresses the application of universal natural laws to daily living, including food selection and preparation. The typical daily healing diet is comprised of 50 percent whole grains and 25 percent vegetables, plus miso soup and assorted condiments, with the occasional presence of fish or fruit. . . .

In 1985, Elinor Levy, Ph.D., and colleagues at the Boston University Medical School's Department of Microbiology published a brief letter in the British medical journal *The Lancet* reporting that macrobiotics seems to have a beneficial effect on ten men with Kaposi's sarcoma, a cancer seen frequently in AIDS patients. Although the men received little or no medical treatment, Levy wrote, "Survival appears to compare very favorably with KS patients in general."

Levy's study eventually expanded to nineteen men, and was described in the book *The Way of Hope* by Tom Monte. By mid-1986, when the average life expectancy for those with KS was twenty-two months after diagnosis, the men in Levy's group lived an average of 25 months. By late 1990, three men had survived six to eight years after diagnosis. . . .

The Value of Good Nutrition

While many nutrition specialists are beginning to subscribe to the notion that AIDS is tied to nutritional deficits, few are willing to speculate on the precise nature of this apparently intimate relationship. At this point, there are simply too many unanswered questions. If AIDS patients lack certain nutrients, will better nutrition stem the progress of the disease or perhaps prevent its spread altogether? If nutrition is a key determinant of immunocompetency, what amounts of which nutrients best arm the body's defenses against the HIV? One by one, the answers are emerging from the nation's clinics and research labs like random pieces in a jigsaw puzzle, awaiting the critical moment when enough pieces are in place to suddenly reveal the picture.

But if the revelation is not yet complete, what must be acknowledged is the validity of the quest. Of the thousands of AIDS researchers working feverishly to put an end to this terrible epidemic, not one in ten is investigating nutrition. The vast majority are laboring to develop vaccines and anti-AIDS drugs such as AZT. AZT has shown promise, though the side effects are frequently so painful that patients cannot endure the therapy. Compounding this dilemma was the announcement that the AIDS virus is mutating and becoming resistant to AZT.

Not until the evidence supporting a nutritional link becomes too incontrovertible to brush aside any longer will nutritional therapies gain new respectability, and the hope carried by this promising approach will spread afresh. For the thousands of souls with AIDS, and the many more who will soon be infected, we must hope the revolution comes swiftly.

"Because Western medicine has no 'magic bullets' to fire at the AIDS virus, there is room in the arsenal for herbal remedies, acupuncture, and meditation."

Oriental Medicine Can Help Treat AIDS

Heidi Ziolkowski

Author Heidi Ziolkowski is a journalism professor at California State University at Long Beach. In the following viewpoint, Ziolkowski contends that the limited AIDS treatments produced by the federal government and the pharmaceutical companies have been ineffective. As a result, she argues, many people with AIDS are experimenting with alternative treatments such as meditation, acupuncture, and herbal remedies. These treatments, Ziolkowski maintains, have proven to be effective in easing the symptoms of AIDS.

As you read, consider the following questions:

1. According to the author, why could alternative medicine succeed in treating AIDS where more conventional medicine does not?
2. What types of herbal treatment does the author suggest could treat AIDS?
3. How does acupuncture affect AIDS patients, according to Ziolkowski?

Excerpted from Heidi Ziolkowski, "Oriental Medicine Takes On AIDS." Reprinted, with permission, from the February 1991 issue of *East West Natural Health: The Guide to Well-Being*, Box 1200, 17 Station Street, Brookline Village, MA 02147. Subscriptions $24/year. All rights reserved.

I_f AIDS were curable through Western medicine like syphilis is, if it were manageable like diabetes, if it were a disease of those who suffer in silence and make few demands on society for research and treatment, and if it received little media coverage, alternative practitioners most likely would be assuming a far less prominent role than they are. Because Western medicine has no "magic bullets" to fire at the AIDS virus, there is room in the arsenal for herbal remedies, acupuncture, and meditation. Because the one disease-one cure approach of conventional medicine cannot adequately account for a syndrome which is a constellation of many diseases and many symptoms, those who have contracted HIV have begun to seek healing elsewhere, with varying results. One system they are turning to is traditional Chinese medicine.

Chinese and Western Medicine

For AIDS, the Western and the Chinese systems both have much to offer. The former has identified the causal virus and is better at diagnosing HIV (the human immunodeficiency virus); the latter carries with it centuries of clinical experience treating symptom patterns rather than single diseases. That approach is particularly well suited to AIDS, which is a complex of many diseases and many symptoms, few of which are common to all patients.

Though a discussion of AIDS does not occur in the literature of traditional Chinese medicine (TCM), it corresponds to the TCM symptom patterns, or conformations, of *xu lao*, which in translation refers to a class of conditions characterized by fatigue, especially due to repetition or long duration of an activity. This pattern is cited in a text from the first century B.C.E. [Before the Christian Era] as a deficiency of "vital energies" and organ systems. As noted by researcher and TCM practitioner Qingcai Zhang, M.D., in *AIDS and Chinese Medicine*, from a conformational viewpoint, AIDS can be seen as a severe "deficiency" or malfunctioning of the spleen, lungs, and kidneys.

Six-year HIV-positive survivor Marc Bluestein is representative of a growing number of PWAs (persons with AIDS) who are disillusioned with the Western approach to their healing. Even their term of choice to describe themselves—PWAs—rather than "AIDS patients," "sufferers," or "victims" is an indication of their willingness to take active roles in their health and not be cast as helpless spectators in some medical drama of drugs and physical decline.

Bluestein, who runs a Palm Springs "buyers' club" which helps PWAs acquire alternative therapies, says that he has taken a number of herbal formulas over the years. "At one time," says Bluestein, "I didn't know anything about Chinese medicine. I was exposed to only the typical Western medical model, but the conventional AIDS programs at UCLA and USC had nothing to offer me."

A Treatable Disease

He is under the care of Chinese medicine practitioner Melissa Nagel of Rancho Mirage, California, who, like many of her colleagues, sees AIDS as a "manageable chronic viral illness, not a fatal disease." Nagel believes that AIDS eventually will be thought of as diabetes is now, something which, though degenerative over the long term and potentially life-threatening, is treatable and controllable.

"I don't see any reason why I won't survive this illness," Bluestein says. "To hell with statistics! With AIDS, you learn to trust yourself."

Ancient Cures

I feel that every individual who is diagnosed as HIV positive, as having ARC or AIDS, can also get well. First, I feel they should stop the antibiotics, the IV pentamidine, and especially AZT. Let these individuals turn to Holistic Healing and yet keep their doctors for times of extreme need when a little help from medicine may help—for example, medication for pain relief. I really feel in my heart that this illness can be beaten, but our doctors and our hospitals are not yet open to the holistic side of healing. Our society has been brainwashed into Western medicine with all its chemical drugs. Western medicine as we know it is only a couple of hundred years old. But I ask you—how many years have the Chinese been using acupuncture and herbs successfully? *Over two thousand five hundred years!*

Jeffrey Migota in *They Conquered AIDS!*, 1989.

Bob Felt, publisher of Brookline, Massachusetts-based Paradigm Publications, which specializes in books on Oriental philosophy and healing practices, is less cavalier about the importance of "statistics" and takes a more cautious approach. A longtime computer analyst and programmer, he says, "More rigor goes into the design of a commercial invoice than has gone into what some practitioners have proposed for AIDS. The pharmaceutical companies will continue to rule the world unless acupuncturists and Oriental practitioners learn to report clinical experience properly. There are so-called subjective improvements that they have the resources to report responsibly. Being able to say that patients feel better, are keeping up with their lifestyles, staying out of hospitals, buying time—these are worthwhile goals. Sadly, I'm afraid they will be lost in the noise of unsupported reports and the medicine show of hasty, speculative cures.". . .

Where does one go to find traditional Chinese medical therapies for AIDS? Major cities, including New York, Los Angeles, Boston, New Orleans, Santa Fe, Austin, and San Francisco, all have acupuncturists and herbalists who are treating AIDS patients. In rural areas or smaller towns it may be more difficult to find alternative health care; AIDS activist organizations in urban centers can supply names and addresses of clinics and practitioners administering TCM therapies.

The more complex issue concerns the value of TCM and related treatments. By its very nature, TCM focuses on the subjective, yet those who ask for verification are demanding objectivity. This means scientific accuracy, precision, and repeatability, which, in turn, means generously funded research.

Subhuti Dharmananda, director of the Portland, Oregon-based Institute for Traditional Medicine, says that TCM is in a catch-22 position: critics demand scientific studies and hard data, yet they are unwilling to fund such efforts. "A well-controlled study needs money," Dharmananda says, "and nobody has stepped forth with enough to put together a well-controlled study."

Daniel Hoth, M.D., director of the AIDS division of the National Institute for Allergy and Infectious Diseases, the leading federal agency in AIDS research, said he knew of no work being done with any Chinese herbs by the institute. "Research is funded by applying for grants, and it is tough competition," Hoth says. Though applications by researchers other than those working at established Western medical schools and universities "would not be rejected out of hand," Hoth could not cite a single instance in which such an application had ever been approved.

"There's an overall bias that nothing good comes out of China—only out of Washington and big American cities," says Martin Delaney, co-founder and co-director of the San Francisco-based AIDS awareness and activism organization Project Inform.

Compound Q

One of the most promising treatments for HIV infection, however, had its origins in Chinese folk medicine, not in Western medical research centers. Trichosanthin, an extract of the Chinese herb *Trichosanthes kirilowii*, used for over two decades in China to induce abortion, has been available in this country since 1987 under the name GLQ223 (Compound Q) for laboratory, clinical, and self-administration studies. Delaney called Q "the most effective drug we've seen" at killing HIV-infected cells.

Unlike conventional AZT treatment for AIDS, proponents of

trichosanthin say that it is cell-specific, killing only infected cells and leaving healthy cells unharmed. This is a major advantage, since the immune systems of HIV-infected persons are already severely damaged, and any additional damage can be life-threatening.

"I feel like there's a light at the end of the tunnel," says James Beale, an Oakland, California, PWA and AIDS activist who has used Q intravenously and has experimented with rectal and sublingual (under-the-tongue) administration. "Compound Q has put my situation on hold. I'm not getting any worse and I'm even getting a little better. I'm not ready to say it's solved the problem, but it's part of the solution."

Data released in May 1990 would seem to bolster Beale's optimism, since eight of sixty-two long-term Q-users have "graduated" from a San Francisco treatment program administered by Project Inform. In Delaney's words, "There's nothing in their blood work that suggests that anything is wrong with these people." They have been "invited" to go off all further treatment, "not because we think that they're cured," Delaney says, "but because we don't know what this means." The best way to find out is to determine how they do without treatment.

Compound Q, however, is no simple herbal tea. A highly purified and concentrated extract, it is akin to chemotherapy, and, as such, it can produce side effects ranging from fever and muscle aches to severe allergic reactions and even coma or death. Delaney cautions, "It's dangerous stuff. You can't fiddle with it at home in your kitchen."

Approximately 1,000 American PWAs have tried Compound Q or the Chinese product, trichosanthin. Compound Q is still in the test stages and will not receive approval by the U.S. Food and Drug Administration for several years, if indeed it ever does. At present it is legally available only to those participating in clinical studies, such as through community-based treatment programs in Miami, New York, San Francisco, and Los Angeles. Some PWAs have begun to self-administer the Chinese counterpart of Q after obtaining it through the "AIDS underground," which makes new and often controversial treatments available to those who do not have time to wait for FDA approval. Ingesting the raw herb *Trichosanthes kirilowii* in lieu of Q is not a viable option, however, since the active ingredient, trichosanthin, is not present in sufficient quantity in the unpurified form to have any effect on the AIDS virus.

Traditional Chinese Medicines

Broadly, traditional Chinese medicine strategies for treating HIV infection fall into the following categories: herbs to reduce the potency of the AIDS virus; herbs to rebuild the HIV-damaged immune system; herbs that treat specific AIDS-related opportunistic infections and malignancies; therapies, such as acupuncture, moxibustion, and gi gong breathing exercises, which relieve nonspecific symptoms; and herbs that lessen the adverse side effects of Western medications, such as anemia caused by the use of AZT.

In cooperation with Misha Cohen of the San Francisco AIDS Alternative Healing Project, Qingcai Zhang of the Oriental Healing Arts Institute began, in March 1988, a six-month clinical trial of herbal therapy for AIDS patients. This work has continued in the Los Angeles area, especially at Integrated Health Services in Lakewood. Zhang has treated more than 150 PWAs with the thirty-eight herbal formulas he designed and modified according to Cohen's clinical observations.

Beneficial Results from Acupuncture

Experimental studies show that there are definite effects on the immune function by acupuncture. If a drug was found to have these beneficial results with no side-effects, doctors would surely be clamoring to use it.

Acupuncture has been used to treat addiction and a wide variety of health problems in Europe and the USA for some 25 years, and disease in general in China and Japan for thousands of years. Orthodox medicine may ignore its potential but the public will not. Indeed, its usefulness in the treatment of AIDS is proving its enormous potential.

Leon Chaitow and Simon Martin, *A World Without AIDS*, 1988.

Practitioners throughout the country are using these formulas in their practices with good results. New Orleans nutritionist and health advocate Orisia Haas treats seventy PWAs with Zhang's herbal formulas, consulting with him several times each week to adjust doses. "I'm getting wonderful results," Haas said. "Some of my patients are completely off medication and doing beautifully." In those patients who choose to remain on AZT, she said, "The herbs mitigate the [side] effects of the medication, as well as the disease process itself."

Zhang's selection of herbs was based in part on pharmacological work done at the Chinese University of Hong Kong and the University of California, Davis. Researchers found eleven Chinese herbs that inhibited HIV production in the test tube. Based on these findings, as well as on an extensive review of current and ancient herbal literature, Zhang designed three groups of formulas: those immune-enhancing formulas directed at the suppression of HIV; those formulas for nonspecific complaints, such as night sweats, low-grade fevers, lethargy, and weight loss; and those designed specifically for opportunistic diseases.

Much of Zhang's most dramatic success has been with the third category. Viral infections, such as herpes, Epstein-Barr virus, and cytomegalovirus, are common in PWAs, as are fungal infections such as candidiasis, myobacterial infections such as tuberculosis, and protozoal infections such as *Pneumocystis carinii* pneumonia. Such opportunistic diseases are rare, or at least not life-threatening, in healthy persons with intact immune systems. "It is the opportunistic diseases that kill people," Zhang says. "No one dies [just] because he has the [AIDS] virus."

Of Zhang's formulas, one of the most promising, and one of the most commonly used, consists of viola (*Viola yedoensis*), epimedium (*Epimedium grandiflorum*), licorice (*Glycyrrhiza uralensis*), coptis (*Coptis sinensis*), prunella (*Prunella vulgaris*), astragalus (*Astragalus membranaceus*), and cassia seed (*Cassia tora*). Of these herbs, the first three have exhibited inhibitory effects on HIV in laboratory studies. Specifically, Japanese researchers have found that glycyrrhizin, the active component of licorice, appears to prevent an HIV infection from progressing to the symptomatic stage. Astragalus is an immune-regulating herb used in China as a tonic, and coptis has proved effective against oral thrush, a common fungal infection in PWAs. . . .

Immune System Cells

The most frequently discussed of the laboratory tests is the T4-cell count, usually referred to as simply the T-cell count. The normal average reading for an HIV-negative person is around 1000. T-cells are immune system cells that become infected with HIV. A count of healthy T-cells for PWAs is analogous to the blood-sugar readings diabetics take to monitor their control. Both tests indicate the patient's condition at the time of the test but do not convey the patient's status over time. T-cell counts thus can be misleading, since the counts of anyone, HIV positive or not, can fluctuate, especially when the person is under stress, as is certainly the case with those who are HIV-infected. T-cell levels below 100 are usually seen in terminal stages of the disease, although Nagel says she has patients whose T-cell counts are zero but who are still able to work full time.

"Lab work regarding T-cells is depressing," says Brian McKenna, acupuncturist and co-founder of the Austin Immune Health Clinic in Austin, Texas. "I question T-cell profiles as markers of either sickness or health. It's far more important that patients develop a positive attitude toward their health than it is to document their health via a battery of lab tests."

McKenna and other acupuncturists point to the improved emotional well-being, increased energy levels, and long-term survival of their patients as signs of efficacy. McKenna, who has treated over 200 PWAs, 60 percent of them for a year and a half or longer, has fifteen patients under his care who have been HIV positive for eight to ten years.

Michael Smith, a psychiatrist who treats intravenous-drug users and AIDS patients with acupuncture at Lincoln Hospital in the Bronx, agrees with McKenna that T-cell counts "are not terribly relevant."

"If lab markers were a definitive sign of a patient's health, I'd have buried half my patients by now," says Smith. "I cannot think of a single case of a clear and consistent correlation between T-cells going up and the patient's overall health.

"[Besides,] I'm working with a city-hospital budget. I can't afford to do regular lab tests. One could wish that certain lab markers would [signal] a degree of improvement . . . but the most important question is, Are they still alive?" . . .

Ted Kaptchuk, perhaps best known for *The Web That Has No Weaver*, a book that has become a classic introduction to TCM, expresses some concerns. "Any intervention gives hope, and hope can bring about improvement," he says. "I'm just saying that I don't know if the improvement can be linked to the efficacy of the herbs or to the enthusiasm of the practitioner."

Kaptchuk directed an alternative healing project that treated, among others, AIDS patients, at Lemuel Shattuck Hospital in Jamaica Plain, Massachusetts, for several years, yet he remains skeptical of what Chinese medicine can specifically do for AIDS. Throughout history, he says, there have been "many major plagues, but what has been shown is that Chinese medicine is largely helpless when faced with pestilent diseases. What the practitioners found is that all the people died, regardless of whether they had 'yang or yin deficiencies.' . . . Anyone who says that Oriental medicine has an answer to AIDS is not taking notice of history."

Recognizing Statements That Are Provable

We are constantly confronted with statements and generalizations about social and moral problems. In order to think clearly about these problems, it is useful if one can make a basic distinction between statements for which evidence can be found and other statements which cannot be verified or proved because evidence is not available, or the issue is so controversial that it cannot be definitely proved.

Readers should be aware that magazines, newspapers, and other sources often contain statements of a controversial nature. The following activity is designed to allow experimentation with statements that are provable and those that are not.

The following statements are taken from the viewpoints in this chapter. Consider each statement carefully. *Mark P for any statement you believe is provable. Mark U for any statement you feel is unprovable because of the lack of evidence. Mark C for any statements you think are too controversial to be proved to everyone's satisfaction.*

If you are doing this activity as a member of a class or group, compare your answers with those of other class or group members. Be able to defend your answers. You may discover that others will come to different conclusions than you do. Listening to the reasons others present for their answers may give you valuable insights in recognizing statements that are provable.

P = *provable*
U = *unprovable*
C = *too controversial*

1. Treatment with AZT can prolong the lives of people with AIDS.

2. Since 1987, the survival rate of people with AIDS has increased.

3. AZT is the sole reason that people who contract AIDS are living longer after they are diagnosed.

4. White men survive longer after being diagnosed with AIDS than do women and minorities.

5. The pharmaceuticals industry designs and develops drugs that effectively treat white men, but are less effective in treating women and minorities.

6. Researchers are conducting studies on the effects of diet and nutrition on the immune system.

7. AZT has been known to cause severe side effects including anemia, severe headaches, nausea, and muscular pain.

8. Studies have shown that people under stress have lower immune system responses than do people who are not under stress.

9. Positive thinking can help people with AIDS improve both their emotional and their physical state.

10. Improving the nutritional habits of people with AIDS may help them overcome some of the opportunistic infections associated with AIDS.

11. Nutritional therapies such as lecithin, derived from egg yolk, can effectively treat diseases associated with AIDS.

12. Poor nutrition contributes to the early onset and the seriousness of AIDS.

13. A macrobiotic diet can boost the immune function and the emotional health of people with AIDS.

14. Early diagnosis and treatment of AIDS can help extend the lives of people with AIDS.

15. Many people have turned to various alternative treatments for AIDS because a single cure is unavailable.

16. Traditional Chinese medicine helps AIDS patients live longer than those who subscribe to conventional medicine.

17. Many doctors who treat people with AIDS are becoming more tolerant of alternative treatments.

18. AIDS should be treated as a chronic, manageable, viral disease rather than a fatal one.

19. Many people who contract AIDS overcome their feelings of despair and continue to live happy, productive lives.

Periodical Bibliography

The following articles have been selected to supplement the diverse views presented in this chapter.

Niro Markoff Asistent — "Why I Survive AIDS," *New Age Journal*, September/October 1991. Available from PO Box 53275, Boulder, CO 80321-3275.

Robert Bazell — "Vaccination Market," *The New Republic*, July 1, 1991.

Gene Bylinsky — "A Promising New Assault on AIDS," *Fortune*, February 26, 1990.

Geoffrey Cowley, Mary Hager, and Ruth Marshall — "AIDS: The Next Ten Years," *Newsweek*, June 25, 1990.

Brian Hecht — "Out of Joint," *The New Republic*, July 15 & 22, 1991.

Deanna Hodgin — "Desperate to Live," *Insight*, September 16, 1991.

Terrence Monmaney — "The Return of AZT," *Discover*, January 1990.

Mary Morton — "Surviving AIDS," *East West*, January 1991. Available from Box 1200, 17 Station St., Brookline Village, MA 02147.

Mireya Navarro — "Into the Unknown: AIDS Patients Test Drugs," *The New York Times*, February 29, 1992.

Robert O'Boyle — "Experimenting with Marijuana," *Liberty*, September 1991. Available from Liberty Publishing, 1532 Sims Way, #1, Port Townsend, WA 98368.

Brian O'Reilly — "The Inside Story of the AIDS Drug," *Fortune*, November 5, 1990.

Edmund Pellegrino — "Ethics in AIDS Treatment Decisions," *Origins*, January 18, 1990. Available from the Catholic News Service, 3211 4th St. NE, Washington, DC 20017-1100.

Andrew Pollack — "Gene Therapy Gets the Go-Ahead," *The New York Times*, February 14, 1992.

Andrew Purvis — "Forging a Shield Against AIDS," *Time*, April 1, 1991.

Glossary

ACT UP (AIDS Coalition to Unleash Power) An international **AIDS** protest organization. ACT UP has been instrumental in increasing government funding for AIDS and in changing the ways the **FDA** and drug companies test and approve drugs for AIDS treatment. Its methods of protest have been controversial.

aerosol pentamidine A drug used to prevent *pneumocystis carinii* **pneumonia**.

AIDS (acquired immunodeficiency syndrome) A condition characterized by severe weakening of the immune system by **HIV** infection, making one vulnerable to a host of **opportunistic diseases** defined by the Centers for Disease Control.

antibody A protein molecule produced by the body in response to the presence of an **antigen**.

antigen A substance, such as a virus, recognized by the body as foreign and harmful.

antiretroviral A substance that slows or stops the spread of a **retrovirus** like **HIV**.

ARC (AIDS-Related Complex) A variety of symptoms, such as recurring fevers, weight loss, and fungal infections of the mouth or throat, that occur in people with **HIV** infection before they are diagnosed as having **AIDS**.

AZT (azidodideoxythymidine, also known as **zidovudine)** An **antiretroviral** drug that delays the onset of **AIDS** in HIV-infected people.

CD 4 (T4 Helper) A type of white blood cell, also known as a T-helper or T4 cell, that helps the body fight off certain infections. **HIV** invades these cells, weakening or destroying them.

ddC (dideoxycitidine) A drug that, like **AZT**, slows the progress of HIV infection. Many people find ddC easier to tolerate than AZT.

ddI (dideoxyinosine) A drug that, like **AZT**, slows the progress of HIV infection.

DNA (deoxyribonucleic acid) The substance from which chromosomes inside the cell nucleus are formed. Sequences of DNA are genes, which order construction of the millions of types of proteins that make up all forms of life.

ELISA test (enzyme linked immunosorbent assay) A test for the presence of **antibodies** to **HIV**.

FDA (Food and Drug Administration) The government organization responsible for testing drugs before they are approved for sale to the public.

HIV (human immunodefiency virus) a **retrovirus** widely believed to cause **AIDS**.

IV (intravenous) Performed or occurring within or entering by way of a vein.

Kaposi's sarcoma A type of cancer that is characterized by painless pink and purple skin lesions that are actually tumors on the walls of the lymph vessels.

macrobiotic A life philosophy that includes an extremely restricted diet of whole grains and vegetables. Some people believe that **PWAs** should adopt the diet.

opportunistic diseases Illnesses caused by agents that do not cause illness in people with healthy immune systems.

PCP (*pneumocystis carinii* pneumonia)   A disease caused by a common parasite that grows rapidly in the lungs of people with **AIDS** and is the leading cause of death in **AIDS** patients.

PWA   Person with **AIDS**.

retrovirus   A virus that reproduces by using the reverse of the usual process. Most viruses have **DNA** cores and replicate via **RNA**. Retroviruses, however, reproduce by copying their own **RNA** into the **DNA** of the host cell making it unable to perform normally and eventually destroying it.

RNA (ribonucleic acid)   Strands of molecules that produce enzymes, proteins, and hormones that perform organic functions in the body.

safe sex   Sexual practices that by their nature or because of external protection are not likely to transmit the **HIV**.

seropositive   Having **antibodies** to **HIV** present in the blood.

STDs (sexually transmitted diseases)   Diseases, including syphilis, gonorrhea, and chlamydia, whose primary route of transmission is through sexual intercourse.

Western Blot test   A more accurate test than the **ELISA test** for detecting the presence of specific **HIV antibodies**.

zidovudine   *See* **AZT**.

Organizations to Contact

The editors have compiled the following list of organizations that are concerned with the issues debated in this book. All have publications or information available for interested readers. For best results, allow as much time as possible for the organizations to respond. The descriptions are derived from materials provided by the organizations. This was compiled upon the date of publication. Names, addresses, and phone numbers of organizations are subject to change.

Adolescent AIDS Program
Montefiore Medical Center
Albert Einstein College of Medicine
111 E. 210th St.
Bronx, NY 10467
(212) 920-2179

The only adolescent AIDS clinic in the United States, this program was established to educate teenagers on how to prevent AIDS and to medically treat teens with AIDS. The program offers complete medical evaluations, HIV testing, and pre- and post-test counseling. The clinic provides printed information free of charge.

AIDS Coalition to Unleash Power (ACT UP)
135 W. 29th St., #10
New York, NY 10001
(212) 564-2437

ACT UP is comprised of individuals committed to ending AIDS. They believe that politicians, doctors, and researchers are not doing enough to combat the disease. To improve public awareness of AIDS, ACT UP members meet with government officials, hold protests, distribute medical information, and publish the brochure *ACT UP: The AIDS War and Activism*.

AIDS National Interfaith Network (ANIN)
300 I St. NE, Suite 400
Washington, DC 20002
(202) 546-0807

ANIN is a coalition of religious organizations whose goal is to see that everyone affected by AIDS receives compassion, respect, care, and assistance. The network opposes threats to the civil liberties of AIDS patients, including violations of confidentiality and all forms of prejudice and discrimination. The organization publishes the bimonthly newsletter *Interaction*.

American Civil Liberties Union (ACLU)
132 W. 43rd St.
New York, NY 10036
(212) 944-9800

The ACLU champions the rights set forth in the Declaration of Independence and the U.S. Constitution. It opposes any actions, including testing and contact tracing, that might endanger the civil rights of people with

AIDS. The union's publications include the monthly *Civil Liberties Alert*, the quarterly *Civil Liberties*, and various pamphlets, books, and position papers.

American Red Cross AIDS Education Office
1709 New York Ave. NW, Suite 208
Washington, DC 20006
(202) 434-4074

The American Red Cross, established in 1881, is one of America's oldest public health organizations. Its AIDS education office publishes pamphlets, brochures, and posters containing facts about AIDS. These materials are available at local Red Cross chapters. In addition, many chapters offer videotape services, conduct presentations, and operate speakers' bureaus.

Americans for a Sound AIDS/HIV Policy (ASAP)
PO Box 17433
Washington, DC 20041

ASAP provides education to the public about how AIDS has impacted Americans. It advocates HIV testing, partner notification, compassionate response, treatment development, and access to health care. ASAP publishes *A Guide to Federal Funding for HIV Disease*, the book *Christians in the Age of AIDS*, the policy guide *The Church's Response to the Challenge of AIDS/HIV*, and the bimonthly newsletter *AIDS/HIV News*.

Centers for Disease Control (CDC)
1600 Clifton Rd. NE
Atlanta, GA 30333
(404) 329-3311

The CDC, established in 1973, is a government agency within the Public Health Service. It is charged with protecting the public health of the nation by providing leadership in the prevention and control of diseases and by responding to public health emergencies. The CDC publishes information about AIDS in the *HIV/AIDS Prevention Newsletter*, and includes updates on the disease in its weekly report *Morbidity and Mortality Weekly Report*.

Center for Women Policy Studies (CWPS)
2000 P St. NW
Washington, DC 20036
(202) 872-1770

The CWPS was the first national policy institute focused specifically on issues affecting the social, legal, and economic status of women. It believes that the government and the medical community have neglected the effect of AIDS on women and that more action should be taken to help women who have AIDS. The center publishes the book *The Guide to Resources on Women and AIDS* and produced the video *Fighting for Our Lives: Women Confronting AIDS*.

Eagle Forum
PO Box 618
Alton, IL 62002
(618) 462-5415

Eagle Forum is dedicated to preserving traditional family values. This organization believes that AIDS is the result of what it deems as immoral sexual practices, such as homosexual and promiscuous sex and intravenous drug use. It publishes the monthly *Phyllis Schlafly Report*, which frequently includes statements on AIDS issues.

Focus on the Family
420 N. Cascade Ave.
Colorado Springs, CO 80903
(719) 531-3400

Focus on the Family is a Christian organization that seeks to strengthen the traditional family in America. It promotes abstinence from sex until marriage as a way for teenagers to avoid AIDS and opposes safe-sex programs. Focus believes that sexual promiscuity and homosexuality have led to AIDS. It publishes a number of materials, including the booklet *Sexual Conduct in the Age of AIDS*, and monthly magazines *Focus on the Family, Physician,* and *Citizen.*

Gay Men's Health Crisis (GMHC)
Publications/Education Department
129 W. 20th St.
New York, NY 10011-0022
(212) 337-1950

The Gay Men's Health Crisis, founded in 1982, provides support services, education, and advocacy for men, women, and children with AIDS. The group produces a cable television news show "Living with AIDS" and publishes *Treatment Issues*, a monthly newsletter of experimental AIDS therapies, and *AIDS Clinical Update*, a quarterly that compiles the latest developments in the research and treatment of the disease.

The Hastings Center
255 Elm Rd.
Briarcliff Manor, NY 10510
(914) 762-8500

Established in 1969, the center is a nonprofit and nonpartisan research and educational organization devoted to ethical problems in biology, medicine, the social sciences, and behavioral sciences. The center frequently publishes articles about AIDS-related topics in its bimonthly journal *The Hastings Center Report.*

Health/PAC — Health Policy Advisory Center
47 W. 14th St., Suite 300
New York, NY 10011-0100
(212) 627-1847

The Health Policy Advisory Center is a nonprofit, public interest group advocating accessible health care for all. Since its founding in 1968, Health/PAC has challenged the medical community to respond to the needs of all Americans, including those with AIDS. Health/PAC works to provide a progressive analysis of U.S. health care policy and practice. It publishes the quarterly *Bulletin*, which often addresses the needs of people with AIDS.

Hemophilia and AIDS/HIV Network for the Dissemination of Information (HANDI)
The National Hemophilia Foundation (NHF)
110 Greene St., Suite 406
New York, NY 10012
(212) 431-8541

HANDI is the information center of the National Hemophilia Foundation. It provides information on hemophilia and AIDS/HIV to the forty state NHF chapters, to the more than two hundred hemophilia treatment centers nationwide, to hemophiliacs, and to others in need of such information. HANDI focuses on collecting and sharing information on AIDS/HIV risk reduction, HIV treatment options, and issues of living with hemophilia and AIDS/HIV. It publishes the newsletter *HANDI Quarterly*.

The Hetrick-Martin Institute (HMI)
401 West St.
New York, NY 10014
(212) 633-8920
(212) 633-8926 (TTY)

HMI is a nonprofit organization that offers a broad range of social services to gay and lesbian adolescents and their families, as well as to all teenagers at high risk for AIDS. HMI sponsors the HIV/Health Services Program, which helps adolescents with HIV or AIDS obtain medical treatment. It publishes the quarterly newsletter *HMI Report Card*.

Human Immuno-Deficiency Virus Eradication (HIVE)
PO Box 808
Vacaville, CA 95696
(707) 448-1710

HIVE believes that AIDS can be spread by casual contact, and that current information on AIDS is therefore misleading. It calls for mandatory testing, contact tracing, and quarantines to stop the spread of AIDS. HIVE publishes the brochure *The Alarming Reality*, which addresses the spread of AIDS. In addition, it provides various magazine articles and pamphlets about AIDS.

Lambda Legal Defense and Education Fund, Inc.
666 Broadway
New York, NY 10012
(212) 995-8585

Through test-case litigation and public education, Lambda works nationally to defend the rights of lesbians, gay men, and people with HIV. Lambda won the first U.S. AIDS discrimination case in 1983. The group has also worked to expand access to AIDS treatments, has challenged insurance limitations, and has lent support and provided information to local organizations. It publishes *AIDS Update* periodically and the *Lambda Update* quarterly.

National Commission on Acquired Immune Deficiency Syndrome
1730 K St. NW, Suite 815
Washington, DC 20006
(202) 254-5125

The fifteen-member commission was established by Congress in 1989 to make recommendations to Congress and the president concerning a national policy on AIDS and the human immunodeficiency virus (HIV) epidemic. The commission holds public hearings and conducts studies on the problems associated with AIDS. The commission has published two reports, *America Living with AIDS* and *HIV Epidemic in Puerto Rico*.

National Institute of Allergies and Infectious Diseases (NIAID)
Office of Communications
National Institutes of Health
9000 Rockville Pike
Bethesda, MD 20892

NIAID, a government agency, is a research and education institute that focuses on infectious diseases, including AIDS. NIAID publishes materials on AIDS including the booklet *Understanding the Immune System* and the fact sheet *Where Do AIDS Drugs Come From? Drug Discovery, Drug Development, and Clinical Trials*.

People with AIDS (PWA) Coalition
31 W. 26th St.
New York, NY 10010
(212) 532-0290
(800) 828-3280

People with AIDS Coalition provides a hotline for AIDS treatment information and peer counseling for those with AIDS. The coalition publishes *PWA Newsline*, a monthly magazine containing treatment information, news analysis, and features on people living with AIDS, and *SIDAHora*, a Spanish/English quarterly on AIDS in the Hispanic community.

The Risk Reduction Program
PO Box 54700 #2
Los Angeles, CA 90054
(213) 669-2390

In response to the growing concern about HIV infection among adolescents, the Division of Adolescent Medicine, Children's Hospital Los Angeles, developed the Risk Reduction Program. It operates an HIV prevention program and an AIDS treatment clinic and provides written materials on AIDS.

The Rockford Institute
934 N. Main St.
Rockford, IL 61103
(815) 964-5811

The institute calls for rebuilding moral values and recovering the traditional American family. It believes that AIDS is a symptom of the decline of the traditional family, and that only by supporting traditional families and traditional moral behavior will America rid itself of AIDS. The institute publishes *The Family in America* and *The Religion & Society Report* and various syndicated newspaper articles that occasionally deal with the topic of AIDS.

Ryan White Teen Education Program
c/o Athletes and Entertainers for Kids
PO Box 191, Bldg. B
Gardena, CA 90248-0191
(310) 768-8493

The Ryan White Teen Education Program is an AIDS education program for teenagers. This organization presents assemblies to junior high and high school students free of charge and publishes a quarterly newsletter *Visions*.

San Francisco Interreligious Coalition on AIDS
1049 Market St., Suite 200
San Francisco, CA 94103
(415) 558-7066

The coalition includes more than 250 San Francisco religious congregations, agencies, and individuals involved in helping those with AIDS. It maintains listings of more than 100 AIDS clergy available to hospitals, clinics, and service agencies and provides ongoing training and respite opportunities for those who care for AIDS patients. The coalition is a resource for national and international groups seeking local clergy contacts for those infected with HIV. It publishes the monthly newsletter *Coalesce*.

Bibliography of Books

Jad Adams	*AIDS: The HIV Myth*. New York: St. Martin's Press, 1990.
Nancy J. Alexander, Henry L. Gabelnick, and Jeffrey M. Spieler	*Heterosexual Transmission of AIDS*. New York: Alan R. Liss Inc., 1990.
Dennis P. Andrulis	*Crisis at the Front Line: The Effects of AIDS on Public Hospitals*. New York: Priority Press, 1989.
Gene Antonio	*The AIDS Cover-Up?* San Francisco: Ignatius Press, 1987.
John G. Bartlett and Ann K. Finkbeiner	*The Guide to Living with HIV Infection*. Baltimore: Johns Hopkins University Press, 1991.
Ronald Bayer	*Private Acts, Social Consequences: AIDS and the Politics of Public Health*. New York: The Free Press, 1989.
Michael Callen	*Surviving AIDS*. New York: Harper Collins, 1990.
Center on Women Policy Studies	*The Guide to Resources on Women and AIDS*. Washington, DC: September 1991.
P.T. Cohen, Merle A. Sande, and Paul A. Volberding	*The AIDS Knowledge Base: A Textbook on HIV Disease*. Waltham, MA: Medical Publishing Group, 1990.
Inge B. Corless and Mary Pittman-Lindeman	*AIDS: Principles, Practices, and Politics*. New York: Hemisphere Publishing, 1989.
Lorraine Day	*AIDS: What the Government Isn't Telling You*. Rancho Mirage, CA: Rockford Press, 1991.
Rugh R. Faden, Gail Geller, and Madison Powers	*AIDS, Women, and the Next Generation*. New York: Oxford University Press, 1991.
Elizabeth Fee and Daniel M. Fox, eds.	*AIDS: The Burdens of History*. Berkeley: University of California Press, 1988.
Joseph Feldschuh and Doron Weber	*Safe Blood: Purifying the Nation's Blood Supply in the Age of AIDS*. New York: The Free Press, 1990.
T.C. Fry	*The Great AIDS Hoax*. Washington, DC: Life Sciences Institute, 1989.
Michael Fumento	*The Myth of Heterosexual AIDS*. New York: Basic Books, 1990.
Robert Gallo	*Virus Hunting: AIDS, Cancer, and the Human Retrovirus*. New York: Basic Books, 1991.
Scott Gregory and Bianca Leonardo	*They Conquered AIDS! True Life Adventures*. Palm Springs, CA: Tree of Life Publications, 1989.
Mirko D. Grmek	*History of AIDS: Emergence and Origin of a Modern Pandemic*. Princeton, NJ: Princeton University Press, 1990.
Martin Gunderson, David J. Mayo, and Frank S. Rhame	*AIDS: Testing and Privacy*. Salt Lake City: University of Utah Press, 1989.
Richard J. Howard	*Infectious Risks in Surgery*. Norwalk, CT: Appleton & Lange, 1991.

Patricia Illingworth	*AIDS and the Good Society*. London: Routledge, Chapman, Hall, 1990.
William B. Johnston and Kevin R. Hopkins	*The Catastrophe Ahead: AIDS and the Case for a New Public Policy*. New York: Praeger, 1990.
Helen Singer Kaplan	*The Real Truth About Women and AIDS: How to Eliminate the Risks Without Giving Up Love and Sex*. New York: Simon & Schuster, 1987.
James Kinsella	*Covering the Plague: AIDS and the American Media*. New Brunswick, NJ: Rutgers University Press, 1989.
David L. Kirp	*Learning by Heart: AIDS and Schoolchildren in America's Communities*. New Brunswick, NJ: Rutgers University Press, 1989.
Michio Kushi and Martha C. Cottrell	*AIDS, Macrobiotics, and Natural Immunity*. New York: Japan Publications, 1990.
Sydney J. Lachman	*The Emergent Reality of Heterosexual HIV/AIDS*. South Africa: Lennon Limited, 1991.
John Lauritsen	*Poison by Prescription: The AZT Story*. New York: Asklepios, 1990.
Nancy F. McKenzie, ed.	*The AIDS Reader: Social, Political, Ethical Issues*. New York: Penguin Books, 1991.
William H. Masters, Virginia C. Johnson, and Robert C. Kolodny	*Crisis: Heterosexual Behavior in the Age of AIDS*. New York: Grove Press, 1988.
Vickie M. Mays, George W. Albee, and Stanley F. Schneider	*Primary Prevention of AIDS*. Newbury Park, CA: Sage Publications, 1989.
Heather G. Miller, Charles F. Turner, and Lincoln E. Moses	*AIDS: The Second Decade*. Washington, DC: National Academy Press, 1990.
Barbara A. Misztal and David Moss, eds.	*Action on AIDS: National Policies in Comparative Perspective*. New York: Greenwood Press, 1990.
Tom Monte	*The Way of Hope: Michio Kushi's Anti-AIDS Programs*. New York: Warner Books, 1989.
Eve K. Nichols	*Mobilizing Against AIDS*. Cambridge, MA: Harvard University Press, 1989.
Alan E. Nourse	*AIDS*. New York: Franklin Watts, 1989.
Bruce Nussbaum	*Good Intentions: How Big Business and the Medical Establishment Are Corrupting the Fight Against AIDS*. New York: Atlantic Monthly Press, 1991.
Padraig O'Malley, ed.	*The AIDS Epidemic: Private Rights and the Public Interest*. Boston: Beacon Press, 1989.
David G. Ostrow, ed.	*Behavioral Aspects of AIDS*. New York: Plenum Medical Book Co., 1990.
Bob Owen	*Roger's Recovery from AIDS*. Malibu, CA: DAVAR, 1987.
Cindy Patton	*Inventing AIDS*. New York: Routledge, Chapman, and Hall, 1990.
Steven Petrow, Pat Franks, and Timothy R. Wolfred, eds.	*Ending the HIV Epidemic: Community Strategies in Disease Prevention and Health Promotion*. Santa Cruz, CA: Network, 1990.

Christine Pierce and Donald VanDeVeer	*AIDS: Ethics and Public Policy*. Belmont, CA: Wadsworth Publishing, 1988.
Monroe E. Price	*Shattered Mirrors*. Cambridge, MA: Harvard University Press, 1989.
Enrique T. Rueda and Michael Schwartz	*Gays, AIDS, and You*. Old Greenwich, CT: Devin Adair Co., 1987.
Renee Sabatier	*Blaming Others: Prejudice, Race, and Worldwide AIDS*. Philadelphia: New Society Publishers, 1988.
Jeffrey M. Seibert and Roberta A. Olson	*Children, Adolescents, and AIDS*. Lincoln: University of Nebraska Press, 1989.
Shepherd and Anita Moreland Smith	*Christians in the Age of AIDS*. Wheaton, IL: Victor Books, 1990.
Susan Sontag	*AIDS and Its Metaphors*. New York: Farrar, Straus & Giroux, 1989.
James L. Sorenson et al.	*Preventing AIDS in Drug Users and Their Sexual Partners*. New York: The Guilford Press, 1991.
Robert M. Wachter	*The Fragile Coalition: Scientists, Activists, and AIDS*. New York: St. Martin's Press, 1991.
Sarah Barbara Watstein and Robert Anthony Laurich	*AIDS and Women: A Sourcebook*. Phoenix: Oryx Press, 1991.
Rose Weitz	*Life with AIDS*. New Brunswick, NJ: Rutgers University Press, 1991.

Index

District of Columbia, 104, 107
Dittman, Ralph, 90
DNA, 166, 167, 169
Drager, Laura, 131, 137
Drucker, Ernest, 21
drug abusers
  behaviors of, 137, 138-139
  education about AIDS for, 100
  HIV infection among, 30, 39, 131
    contact tracing would not reduce,
      99
  has increased, 22
  moral issues raised by, 51, 59, 72
  nutritional habits of, 181
  transmission of HIV to non-drug
    users, 23, 34, 131, 138
  see also needle-exchange programs
drug testing, 80
drug treatments for AIDS
  alternatives to, 170, 180, 184, 186,
    192
  AZT, 59-60, 96, 192
    is effective against AIDS, 159-164
    con, 165-170, 186
  Compound Q, 190-191
  for infants, 102, 109-110
  funding for
    is too generous, 31
    con, 56-60
Duesberg, Peter, 166, 167, 169

education about AIDS and HIV
  for teenagers
    should be explicit, 141-148
    should promote abstinence,
      149-153
  is more effective than contact
    tracing, 100
  through contact tracing, 92, 94
  to promote communication between
    sex partners, 120-121
  will not prevent AIDS, 127
  see also prevention of AIDS
Ehrenfeld, Tom, 86
Europe, 35, 132
exercise, 170, 173, 178

families
  AIDS's impact on, 35, 37, 66, 108
  AIDS victims' relations with, 64-65,
    172-173
  enforce morality, 52, 53
  of gay people, 60
  government acts against, 52
Feder, Don, 124
feminists, 50
Ferentes, Donna, 63
Fernandez, Joseph, 127, 142, 145

146
Finkbeiner, Ann K., 171
Florida, 79, 80, 81, 85, 86
Food and Drug Administration,
  166, 167, 169, 170, 191
foster care, 111
Freedom of Information Act, 167
Fumento, Michael, 24, 56, 125

gays. See homosexuals
Gellin, Bruce G., 88
Gertz, Alison, 25, 40-41
God
  and AIDS victims, 72
  and value of human life, 64, 69, 70
  disapproves of homosexuality, 64,
    66
Gonzalez, Roberto, 67
Gould, Robert E., 40
government
  and social order, 52, 53
Graber, Caroline R., 95
Graber, Glenn C., 95
Grumet, Barbara Ruhe, 101

Haight Ashbury Free Clinic, 135
Haitians, 28, 181
Haseltine, William A., 21, 22, 166
health care workers
  suffering from AIDS, 81, 83
    are unlikely to infect patients,
      85-86, 88
  support AIDS testing, 79
  testing of for HIV
    alternatives to, 86-87
    con, 84-89
    harms of, 87-89
    pro, 78-83
    would increase litigation, 88-89
Hebert, James, 181, 182
hemophiliacs, 30, 39, 58, 72, 143
hepatitis B, 79, 80, 81, 82, 83, 87, 97
herbalists. See Chinese medicine
heterosexuals
  AIDS threatens, 17-23, 34, 148
    con, 125
  IV-drug users, 22, 39
  "mainstream," 22-23
    con, 29-30, 40
  minorities, 21, 33
  statistics understate HIV risk to,
    20, 21
Hetrick-Martin Institute for Gay and
  Lesbian Youth, 146, 148
Hill, Anita, 48
Hispanics. See Latinos
HIV (human immunodeficiency
  virus), 128, 188

211

215